THE TRIUMPH OF FORM

THE
TRIUMPH
OF
FORM

A STUDY OF THE LATER MASTERS
OF THE HEROIC COUPLET

by

Wallace Cable Brown

THE UNIVERSITY OF NORTH CAROLINA PRESS
CHAPEL HILL

821
B881

MANUFACTURED IN THE UNITED STATES OF AMERICA
BY THE SEEMAN PRINTERY, INC., DURHAM, N. C.

Preface

THIS STUDY is not, I hope, merely the digest of two others in order to make a third; nor is it one in which, as Dr. Johnson remarked about the Scottish people, every body gets a mouthful, but nobody a meal. It is not intended to be biographical, psychological, or philosophic; and it is historical only in the sense that seven poets are, for the most part, chronologically dealt with and the major characteristics of their work derived from earlier sources as parts of a tradition. If the word "chapters" is substituted for "essays" and for "integrity of poetry" we read "integrity of the heroic-couplet tradition," the following statement of purpose by T. S. Eliot may be taken as a general description of my own:

the problem appearing in these essays, which gives them what coherence they have, is the problem of the integrity of poetry, with the repeated assertion that when we are considering poetry we must consider it primarily as poetry and not another thing.[1]

The emphasis upon the poetry "as poetry and not another thing" manifestly imposes a limitation, but it is, I believe, a generous and especially a wise limitation. Without it I should have to emphasize something else, perhaps the history of ideas or "influences" in literature. Such a change would in effect become another kind of limitation, unless I

[1] *The Sacred Wood*, p. viii.

expanded each chapter into the complete critical biography of a particular poet. In the face of these alternatives, I am constrained to reaffirm Eliot's view as the most genuinely "critical" of them all.

By this I do not mean a criticism of "exclusion," in which a technical or esthetic approach unfolds in a vacuum; for I assume that biography, psychology, and certainly philosophy are at all times present on the periphery of the critical problem (the poem as such). But, on the other hand, it is not necessary to explain that John Gay lost his shirt in the stock market crash of 1721 ("the South Sea bubble") in order to interpret his *Panegyrical Epistle to Mr. Thomas Snow;* its poetic values are within the poem: the irony, humor, and technical excellence. Nor does one need to know that George Crabbe endured a miserable early life in order to appreciate fully the poetry of, say, "Peter Grimes." In some of Crabbe's poems there are, as a matter of fact, a lightness and a Chaucerian humor that belie the traditional details of his life. In general, therefore, I have concentrated on the poetry and let the noncritical chips fall where they may.

By mastery of the heroic couplet I mean not only technical mastery, but also superior achievement in poetic structure and in synthesis of style and content. The approach is therefore two-fold, suggested by the interrelated questions: how well has the poet written the heroic couplet? and how well has he interpreted his subject in this form? In dealing with these crucial questions, I have had to allow the emphasis to shift between them as I have proceeded from poet to poet, depending upon the virtuosity of the poet and the nature of his subject matter. In Gay, for example, there is greater emphasis upon his technical mastery of the couplet; but in Crabbe the emphasis shifts to his management of the short narrative in couplets. Throughout this study I have tried to show how fresh and exciting the achievements of the followers of Dryden and Pope actually are—how, despite the restraints they accepted, they still succeeded in opening up their own "world of fine fabling," which even today is eminently readable.

No follower of Dryden and Pope equaled their amazing virtuosity, and only one—Goldsmith—has received anything like recognition as a major poet. At his best, in parts of *The Deserted Village,* he undoubtedly attains greatness of a kind similar to that of Johnson in *The Vanity of Human Wishes.* Yet in variety of subject matter and couplet style Goldsmith is surpassed by Gay, Churchill, and perhaps Crabbe. This does not mean that they are "greater" poets, but rather that they do more with the heroic couplet. In maintaining an essentially critical approach to each poet, I have had to allow a certain amount of repetition. It has been kept to a minimum, however, and I hope that where it appears it will also be justified by another logical reason for repetition, that of emphasis.

My indebtedness to critics and scholars, in the field and out of it, is manifold and, I suppose, manifest. In both the text and the notes I have tried to record this indebtedness, but the attempt has probably not wholly succeeded; and there remains the imposing array of unconscious or forgotten influences to which any writer is subject. For my general method and particular critical suggestions I am most indebted to the work of T. S. Eliot, Yvor Winters, Mark Van Doren, Geoffrey Tillotson, and Robert Kilburn Root. And for incisive criticism and unflagging encouragement I owe more to Dona Worrall Brown than I can put into words. Finally, I am grateful to Professor Howard Mumford Jones of Harvard and Professors Dougald MacMillan and Richmond P. Bond of the University of North Carolina for their careful reading of the manuscript and their numerous constructive suggestions.

Parts of Chapters I, II, III, and IV have appeared as

articles in various journals, for the permission to reprint which I wish to thank the editors of *College English*, *The University of Kansas City Review*, *Publications of the Modern Language Association*, *The Modern Language Quarterly*, *Studies in Philology*, and *The Journal of English and Germanic Philology*. I also wish to thank the following individuals and publishers for permission to quote from some of their books: Mark Van Doren (*The Poetry of John Dryden*), the Hogarth Press (*Homage to John Dryden* by T. S. Eliot), Faber and Faber (*Selected Poems of Ezra Pound*, ed. T. S. Eliot and *The Use of Poetry and the Use of Criticism* by T. S. Eliot), Methuen and Company (*The Sacred Wood* by T. S. Eliot), William Morrow and Company (*In Defense of Reason* by Yvor Winters), the Oxford University Press (*The Poetical Works of George Crabbe*, ed. A. J. and R. M. Carlyle), and The Macmillan Company (*A Survey of English Literature* by Oliver Elton).

—W. C. B.

University of Kansas City
Kansas City, Missouri
December 16, 1947

Contents

THE TRIUMPH OF FORM

"Where order in variety we see,
And where, though all things differ, all agree."
—*Windsor Forest*

Chapter I

Prologue to the Succession

I

DURING the last three decades the literature of "our indispensable eighteenth century," which Wordsworth deplored and Arnold patronized, has been readmitted to respectability. Neo-classic poetry in particular has been so successfully revaluated by critics like Van Doren, Eliot, Tillotson, and Root[1] that it is no longer possible to take seriously Arnold's dismissal of Dryden and Pope as "classics of our prose." But these two poets have received the lion's share of critical attention. Little has been done about the achievements in neo-classic poetry after Pope, particularly as part of the heroic-couplet tradition.

This tradition was highly centralized, for it is not too much to say that every important use and characteristic of the heroic couplet in the work of Gay, Young, Johnson, Churchill, Goldsmith, Cowper, and Crabbe are in some way foreshadowed in the work of Dryden and Pope. They became therefore the great models who were, in the best neo-classic sense, "imitated" by their eighteenth- and nineteenth-century successors. But in this process of imitation each of the successors, with the exception of Young and Cowper,

[1] Most important of these critical works: Mark Van Doren, *The Poetry of John Dryden;* T. S. Eliot, *Homage to John Dryden* and *John Dryden, the Poet, the Dramatist, the Critic;* F. R. Leavis, *Revaluation;* David Nichol Smith, *Some Observations on Eighteenth Century Poetry;* Edith Sitwell, *Alexander Pope;* Geoffrey Tillotson, *On the Poetry of Pope;* R. K. Root, *The Poetical Career of Alexander Pope.*

impressed his own genius upon the heroic couplet. Thus the traditional form was broadly maintained, but at the same time significantly varied—precisely how varied it will be one of the purposes of this study to show.

Here the question "what is the heroic couplet" naturally arises, and we need at least a working definition of the full-fledged form. No absolute all-inclusive definition is of course possible, yet many have been attempted. Of these I know of none more vivid and satisfactory than Mark Van Doren's, which follows:

This adaptation involved a number of characteristics, of which the end-stop . . . was only one; the others were a conformation of the sentence-structure to the metrical pattern, a tendency towards polysyllables within the line, a tendency towards emphatic words at the ends of lines, and a frequent use of balance with pronounced caesura. The end-stop, and the modification of sentence-structure to suit the length of the measure, made for pointedness if not for brevity, and provided in the couplet a ratiocinative unit which served admirably as the basis for declarative or argumentative poems. The polysyllables made for speed and flexibility, and encouraged a latinized, abstract vocabulary. The insistence upon important words for the closing of lines meant that the sense was not likely to trail off or be left hanging. And the use of balance promoted that air of spruce finality with which every reader of Augustan verse has long been familiar.[2]

Of all the later masters of the heroic couplet Gay is closest to Pope, but in description he is more realistic and in satire he lacks Pope's biting malice. Johnson is deeper and more original than Gay; yet he too exploits one aspect of Pope's achievement: the forcing of the didactic-satiric poem into lyrical territory. In Churchill we encounter the influence of Dryden, but that of Pope is no less important; for "the triumph of irony" in Churchill is the culmination of another aspect of Pope, most apparent in his ironic epistle

[2] *Op. cit.*, p. 73.

To Augustus. In Goldsmith we move from the realm of satire into that of non-satiric portraiture and social discussion, which of course is still another aspect of Pope—the Pope of the *Essay on Man* and the non-satiric epistles. The couplet, however, becomes more mellow and the mood more sentimental, with the most pronounced emphasis of all upon the lyrical impulse. Finally, in Crabbe both Dryden and Pope reappear—Dryden in Crabbe's use of the triplet and alexandrine and in his restriction of the couplet to narrative, Pope in a dozen technical characteristics, including the medial caesura, a high degree of balance and antithesis, predominantly masculine rhymes, and a fondness for epigram.

Although Dryden and Pope left their mark indelibly upon the couplet, they were not the only begetters of the form, for its use antedates Dryden by many years. From beginning to end, the heroic couplet has the longest consecutive history of any major stanzaic form in English. It was a living form, regularly used by important poets, for almost two hundred years—from Waller's earliest poem in the 1620's to Crabbe's *Tales of the Hall* in 1819. There are, of course, many historical reasons (social, biographical, psychological) for this supremacy of the couplet. But the reasons which concern us here are technical and esthetic. As Yvor Winters has pointed out,[3] the couplet is the strictest and most limited of all verse forms. Although not usually so considered, it is the smallest possible stanza: the next step must be blank verse. Since it is the most rigid poetic form, it is the one from which the greatest variations are possible without destroying the basic pattern. The variations in technique and usage in Dryden and Pope and in the five masters of the form who followed them point to one reason why the heroic couplet was so attractive to so many poets of great talent for so long a time.

[3] *In Defense of Reason:* "What, then, makes the couplet so flexible? The answer can be given briefly: its seeming inflexibility": p. 141.

If the critics have given us a series of masterful studies of Dryden and Pope, the literary historians, who have been active in the field much longer, have revealed, among other things, the antecedents of the heroic couplet. Dryden and Pope had named Edmund Waller and Sir John Denham as their chief literary ancestors. The results of modern investigation, however, have considerably altered this genealogy.[4] It now appears certain (1) that in singling out Waller and Denham, Dryden indicates only an end-link in the early development of the heroic couplet; (2) that the real beginnings of the form must be attributed to the Elizabethans, particularly Nicholas Grimald, Thomas Heywood, Marlowe, Hall, and Drayton; and (3) that in moulding the form the Latin distich was probably most influential.[5]

In the early seventeenth century the development of the heroic couplet continued, especially in the work of Jonson, Sandys, and Falkland, whose couplet poems, as Miss Wallerstein has shown, are contemporaneous with and little inferior to those of Waller and Denham.[6]

By 1640 this early form of the heroic couplet had become a fixture in English occasional verse. At this time Waller and Denham were also using the form, although

[4] See Henry Wood, "The Beginnings of the Classical Heroic Couplet," *AJP*, XI, 55-79; Felix W. Schelling, "Ben Jonson and the Classical School," *PMLA*, XIII, 221-50; J. S. P. Tatlock, "The Origin of the Closed Couplet in English," *The Nation*, XCIII, N.S., 390; C. E. Knowlton, "The Origin of the Closed Couplet in English," *ibid.*, 134; Arthur M. Clark, "Thomas Heywood's *Art of Love* Lost and Found," *The Library*, 4th Series, III, 210-22; George P. Shannon, "Nicholas Grimald's Heroic Couplet and the Latin Elegiac Distich," *PMLA*, XLV, 532-42; Ruth Wallerstein, "The Development of the Rhetoric and Metre of the Heroic Couplet, Especially in 1625-1645," *PMLA*, L, 166-210; George Williamson, "The Rhetorical Pattern of Neo-Classical Wit," *MP*, XXXII, 55-82.

[5] Chaucer can, I believe, be safely left out of the picture. His couplet "was lost in the metrical and linguistic confusion of fifteenth century England," and, in any case, the closed and balanced couplet in his style is the exception, for he tends to use an "oblique" rather than a "parallel" syntax: see Shannon, *op. cit.*, p. 532; Mary A. Hill, "Rhetorical Balance in Chaucer's Poetry," *PMLA*, XLII, 845-62; and W. K. Wimsatt, Jr., "One Relation of Rhyme to Reason," *MLQ*, V, 323-39.

[6] Wallerstein, *op. cit.*, pp. 186-210; see also Kurt Weber, *Lucius Carey, Second Viscount Falkland*, pp. 118-36 and 275-300.

neither had as yet published the poems that were to establish them in the tradition. In 1642 appeared the first (unauthorized) version of *Cooper's Hill* by Denham; but much earlier Waller had written such poems as "Of the Danger His Majesty Escaped in the Road at St. Andero" (c. 1623), "On the Taking of Sallè" (c. 1632), "Upon His Majesty's Reparing of St. Paul's" (c. 1633), and "The Countess of Carlisle in Mourning" (c. 1636)—all in early heroic couplets. Waller and Denham did not so much add anything to the tradition of heroic verse as consolidate and limit its development.[7] They wrote in this form so consistently and, at their best, so well that they have received undue credit as the founders of the whole movement.

The extent and nature of Waller's achievements appear characteristically in his early poem, "The Battle of the Summer Islands." Almost 90 per cent of its 220 lines contain a central caesura, nearly half of which are after the fourth syllable.[8] Such uniformity points ahead to the practice of Dryden and to the Pope formula in his famous letter to Walsh.[9] Similar uniformity occurs in the number of stresses per line, which are overwhelmingly divided between five and four (110 and 106 lines respectively, with only four lines of six stresses).[10] In a surprising number of instances there appear trochaic substitutions in the first metrical foot—forty-seven out of the 220 lines. Also, with few exceptions, the couplets are fully end-stopped. Finally, parallel syntactic structures predominate, of the kind illustrated by the following passage:

[7] "In consequence of such tendencies of wit and verse, Waller must appear not as an inventor but rather as a consolidator of poetic development and as the acknowledged leader of a restrictive movement": Williamson, "The Rhetorical Pattern of Neo-Classical Wit," p. 73.

[8] The figures are: 2nd syllable, 3 lines; 3rd, 1; 4th, 107; 5th, 66; 6th, 24; 7th, 10; 8th, 7; and 9th, 2.

[9] In *The Works of Alexander Pope*, ed. Elwin and Courthope, VI, 56-59.

[10] Suppression of one or more accents occurs where the scansion calls for a stress, but the unimportance of meaning at that point will not allow it: see Root, *op. cit.*, pp. 32-50.

> For the kind spring, which but salutes us here,
> Inhabits there, and courts them all the year.
> Ripe fruits and blossoms on the same trees live;
> At once they promise what at once they give.
> So sweet the air, so moderate the clime,
> None sickly lives, or dies before his time.
> Heaven sure has kept this spot of earth uncursed,
> To show how all things were created first.   (40-47)

The first three couplets are rigidly balanced, with the thought moving between similarity and contrast throughout. Note, for example, the contrast between "but salutes us here" and "Inhabits there"; the syntactic and thought parallel in the line, "At once they promise what at once they give"; and the complete contrast and balance of the third couplet. In terms of the entire passage, the last couplet is a summary and conclusion of all that goes before.

In addition to these technical characteristics, "The Battle of the Summer Islands" anticipates Dryden and Pope in that it is mock-heroic. Although manifestly inferior to *Mac-Flecknoe* and *The Rape of the Lock*, it does treat in heroic style a relatively insignificant episode—a "battle" between the islanders and two whales cast upon the shore by a storm. The opening couplets, appealing to the muses and echoing Virgil, clearly strike the mock-heroic note:

> Aid me, Bellona! while the dreadful fight
> Betwixt a nation and two whales I write.
> Seas stain'd with gore I sing, advent'rous toil!
> And how these monsters did disarm an isle . . .

Also epic-like, the poem is divided into three cantos; and the tone of light humorous mockery is maintained throughout, suggested most clearly in the concluding couplets of the first two cantos:

> But while I do these pleasing dreams indite,
> I am diverted from the promised fight.

> But how they fought, and what their valour gain'd,
> Shall in another Canto be contain'd.

A later and better poem by Waller, "On St. James's Park, as Lately Improved by His Majesty," reveals further characteristics of the early heroic couplet. First, the special kind of neo-classic wit, which George Williamson has described, appears full-fledged in this poem. It was called the "turn" because "the 'points' of this wit generally depend upon antithesis, open or veiled, which provides an unexpected turn of thought."[11] In the "turn," which is of course a distant cousin of the metaphysical conceit, the domination of "judgment" over "fancy" (imagination) is almost complete. In this passage,

> The ladies, angling in the crystal lake,
> Feast on the waters with the prey they take;
> At once victorious with their lines, and eyes,
> They make the fishes, and the men, their prize, (33-36)

the "turn" develops fully in the second couplet, in which the antithetic points of the wit move between "lines"–"fishes" and "eyes"–"men." But the thought relationships are more complex than this, for within the couplet "lines" and "eyes" are parallel to "fishes" and "men"; and between the lines "victorious" and "prize" are related as cause-and-effect. Finally, the two couplets are bound together in that the "prey" for which the ladies angle are the men as well as the fishes, both of which become their "prize."

Within individual lines of this poem may be found the simplest parallel structures of the heroic couplet, as well as some of the more complicated variations. Thus the balanced line of four stresses, with the medial accent suppressed and the two halves identical in syntax:

[11] "The Rhetorical Pattern of Neo-Classical Wit," p. 65; see also George Williamson, *The Donne Tradition*, pp. 213-25; and *The Poetical Works of Sir John Denham*, ed. T. H. Banks, pp. 30-31.

> To make a river than to build a town.   (12)

> His manly posture, and his graceful mien   (59)

> Of rising kingdoms, and of falling states.   (122)

In the last line, thought contrast is added to syntactic balance. A more complicated structure appears when the medial accent is not suppressed because it falls on an important word, which in the following line is a verb:

> Whose loaded branches hide the lofty mound.   (46)

A still greater complexity develops when the balance is subtly disturbed by an unexpected inversion in word order:

> They bathe in summer, and in winter slide.   (24)

The formula "bathe in summer" requires "slide in winter" for perfect balance. It is noteworthy too that the thought in the balanced phrases is in contrast. For the most part, the metrical structure of this poem is iambic with variations; but occasionally a line will deviate too far from this norm, as in the following:

> Tempers hot July with December's frost,   (52)

in which the majority of the metrical feet (the first three) are trochaic.

Finally, as is characteristic of the later management of heroic verse, the couplets, although wholly end-stopped, are often united into groups by parallel syntax. Thus lines 20-29 are bound together by the two-fold repetition of a "methinks" construction:

> Methinks I see the love that shall be made . . .   (21)

> Methinks I hear the music in the boats . . .   (25)

And a similar kind of syntax unifies the following couplets:

> In such green palaces the first kings reign'd,
> Slept in their shades, and angels entertain'd;

> With such old councellors they did advise,
> And, by frequenting sacred groves, grew wise.
>
> (71-74)

Although Waller's technical contributions to the heroic couplet were less extensive than his influence, he did much to limit and fix the form. By writing so consistently in this form, he gave it currency, and so provided (along with Denham) a practice that Dryden could look back to as an established tradition.

Compared to Waller, Denham is a one-poem poet; and just as he concentrated all his talents on *Cooper's Hill,* so his achievement is greater than Waller's in any single poem. Although by no means a great poem, *Cooper's Hill* provides one formula for the occasional poem in heroic verse. And in it Denham deserves credit for having invented a genre: the panoramic-reflective poem in which nature description is intermingled with philosophic contemplation. *Cooper's Hill* begot a long line of descendents, and was astonishingly famous for more than a century.[12]

In *Cooper's Hill* may be found regularly the same characteristics of the early heroic couplet that Waller employs. There is, for example, the same antithetic structure:

> Is there no temperate Region can be known,
> Betwixt their Frigid, and our Torrid Zone?
>
> (139-40)

> While driness moysture, coldness heat resists,
> All that we have, and that we are, subsists.
> While the steep horrid roughness of the Wood
> Strives with the gentle calmness of the flood.
>
> (207-10)

The last two couplets are also bound together by the syntactic repetition of the "while" constructions. The entire poem is

---

[12] See *The Poetical Works of Sir John Denham,* ed. Banks, pp. 55-57 and 333-41; and R. A. Aubin, *Topographical Poetry in XVIII-Century England,* pp. 33-114.

written in predominantly end-stopped, caesuraed, and five- or four-stress couplets.

Since the basic structure is parallel rather than oblique, the couplet norm tends to assert itself at the expense of larger unities. This is, of course, characteristic of neo-classic poetry in general. Denham counteracts this epigrammatic tendency in ways which were more successfully exploited by the later masters of heroic verse. One of these ways is the use of parenthesis:

> No wonder, if (advantag'd in my flight
> By taking wing from thy auspicious height)
> Through untrac'd ways, and aery paths I fly,
> More boundless in my Fancy than my eie.   (9-12)

The thought beginning "No wonder, if" of the first couplet is suspended until, and made dependent upon, the second couplet by the intervening parenthesis. Another device is the occasional use of enjambment placed solidly within a context of closed couplets:

> But his proud head the aery Mountain hides
> Among the Clouds; his shoulders, and his sides
> A shady mantle cloaths; his curled brows
> Frown on the gentle stream, which calmly flows,
> While winds and storms his lofty forehead beat:
> The common fate of all that's high or great.   (217-22)

The dozen couplets which precede and follow this passage are rigidly end-stopped, so the first two above are, in effect, united by enjambment. But the run-on lines are not wholly free, because of the importance, in meaning and stress, of the rhyme words, two of which are nouns and two verbs. Technically the passage is characteristic of Denham's placing of the caesura after the fourth, fifth, or sixth syllable and of his variations between four and five stresses to the line.

The thought of this passage illustrates the descriptive-philosophic nature of the whole poem, which set a precedent through Pope for the later masters of the heroic couplet. The mountain is portrayed in the first five lines; then in the last line the entire picture is suddenly interpreted philosophically in terms of human heights and greatness: just as the mountain, which lifts its proud head into the clouds above the river, must withstand the beating of storms against its "lofty forehead," so men who achieve greatness must expect "the bludgeonings of fate."

The panoramic quality of *Cooper's Hill* results from Denham's method of procedure. Standing on this hill outside London, he simply looks in various directions and then, in rather generalized language, describes the significant objects in view. Interspersed among the descriptive passages and linked logically to them are the longer passages of philosophic reflection. These are concerned with such subjects as urban versus country life, the history of English kings, criticism of religious lethargy and zeal, the beneficial effects of the river Thames on agriculture and commerce, the privileges and responsibilities of kings, etc. In terms of the poem as a whole, "the nature description is relatively unimportant, being to a large extent conventional or vaguely general, and serving merely as a peg on which to hang ethical and philosophical reflections."[13] It is also worth noting that Waller's couplets "On St. James's Park, as Lately Improved by His Majesty" follow this same panoramic formula for the purpose of philosophic reflection.

The famous "turn" with which *Cooper's Hill* opens is a model for this kind of neo-classic wit, but as poetry and as wit it is less effective than Denham's equally famous apostrophe to the river Thames:

> O could I flow like thee, and make thy stream
> My great example, as it is my theme!
> Though deep, yet clear, though gentle, yet not dull,
> Strong without rage, without ore-flowing full.   (189-92)

[13] *Denham*, ed. Banks, p. 48.

The two couplets are logically related in that the second is a specific elaboration of the general idea in the first, a practice characteristic of Johnson and Goldsmith later. Within the first couplet the thought and structure are parallel; within the second, sharply antithetic. The "turn" occurs in the second couplet, where it slowly unfolds through the thought contrasts signalized by the connectives "though," "yet," and "without."

Finally, as an indication of increasing balance and antithesis in the couplet, we may briefly examine Denham's short poem "On the Earl of Strafford's Tryal and Death." This poem exists in two versions, written twenty years apart (1641-1661); the earlier version contains twenty, the later thirty, lines. Most significant are the later additions, particularly the following sentence of six lines:

> Now private pity strove with publick hate,
> Reason with Rage, and Eloquence with Fate:
> Now they could him, if he could them forgive;
> He's not too guilty, but too wise to live;
> Less seem those Facts which Treasons Nick-name bore,
> Than such a fear'd ability for more.   (17-22)

In the first two of these couplets, every line is strictly balanced; and each half presents a thought contrast with its counterpart. The third couplet is balanced between its two lines, which contrast in music and movement, the first being slow and weighty with five stresses, the second quick and nervous, with only four stresses. Because of these additions and other minor changes, the later version of the poem represents a much closer approximation to the fully developed norm of heroic verse. And significantly this version was written at a time when Dryden was already practicing for his own great achievements.

II

Because the work of Dryden and Pope moulded and fixed the heroic-couplet tradition, a résumé of their achievements must precede any study of the later masters of the form. In the hands of Dryden the heroic couplet reached maturity; in the hands of Pope it attained its greatest brilliance and perfection. But technically the difference between them and their predecessors was not so much a matter of absolute qualitative superiority as one of completeness and extensiveness of usage.

The most important single contribution that Dryden made to heroic-couplet poetry was to expand its use into areas never before entered by the form and to confirm, by brilliant performance, its use in other areas. All the major kinds of poetry and many minor subdivisions are represented in Dryden's multifarious poetic activity. First there are the twenty-eight plays, most of which were written wholly in couplets. As drama a few of these are respectable, but most of them are second-rate. However, as Van Doren says, "it was in them that he became fully aware of the energy which is latent in the heroic couplet."[14] Next there is Dryden's prodigious composition of narrative verse, almost all of which was translation or adaptation (including Virgil's epic) from classical and other sources. This output accounts for more than two-thirds of his nondramatic poetry, and practically all of it is in heroic couplets. In the third place, we must consider Dryden as a lyric poet, although here the heroic couplet is not so predominant. Finally, in expository verse, with its emphasis on ratiocination, we have Dryden at his best, especially if, as I propose to do, we include in this category his occasional poetry of all kinds.

It was with genuine critical insight that Pope described Dryden's style as "The varying verse, the full resounding line, The long majestic march, and energy divine," for these qualities are among the most important that Dryden added to heroic verse. Although they appear at their best in the prologues, epilogues, and satires, they may be found through-

---

[14] *Op. cit.*, p. 89.

out the better heroic plays. In *Aureng-Zebe*, for example, the queen-mother, Nourmahal, thus responds to a crucial situation involving her two sons and her incestuous love for one of them ("Morat must fall, if Aureng-Zebe should rise"):

> 'Tis true; but who was e'er in love, and wise?
> Why was that fatal knot of marriage tied,
> Which did, by making us too near, divide?
> Divides me from my sex! for Heaven, I find,
> Excludes but me alone of womankind.
> I stand with guilt confounded, lost with shame,
> And yet made wretched only by a name.
> If names have such command on human life,
> Love sure's a name that's more divine than wife.
> That sovereign power all guilt from action takes,
> At least the stains are beautiful it makes.   (III, i)

The couplets move briskly, but the pace is carefully modulated by varying stress, movement, and sound. The first, sixth, and ninth lines, for example, are slow-moving and full five-stress, in contrast to the four-stress faster-moving seventh and eleventh lines. An energetic argumentative tone dominates the entire passage, which is plentifully polysyllabic and which ends with a satisfying "air of spruce finality."

Although Dryden's most effective narratives are the free translations from Boccaccio, Chaucer, and the classics, it was in the heroic plays that he developed his couplet technique for these later performances. And within the satires there are frequent occasions for the use of narrative. *The Hind and the Panther* contains many such passages; *MacFlecknoe* is a mock-epic incident; and *Absalom and Achitophel* is based upon an epic situation, in which the satire is linked together by narrative passages, like the following:

> Strong were his hopes a rival to remove,
> With blandishments to gain the public love,
> To head the faction while their zeal was hot,

And popularly prosecute the plot.
To further this, Achitophel unites
The malcontents of all the Israelites,
Whose differing parties he could wisely join
For several ends to serve the same design;
The best (and of the princes some were such),
Who thought the power of monarchy too much;
Mistaken men and patriots in their hearts,
Not wicked, but seduced by impious arts;
By these the springs of property were bent
And wound so high they cracked the government.

(I, 487-500)

These couplets are in Dryden's best manner, and they fulfill most of the requirements for the mature neo-classic form. They still do not constitute pure narrative, but their speed and firmness (even though end-stopped) give a full narrative effect. At the end of the passage, Achitophel's hopes for success, mentioned at the beginning, have been largely achieved ("they cracked the government"); so there is a clear-cut movement forward. The fast pace of this movement comes from Dryden's use of polysyllabic words, the division of subject, verb, and object between the lines of the couplets, and the suppression of one normal stress in the majority of the lines.

But it is in the *Fables Ancient and Modern* that Dryden's best narrative will be found. In this area his achievements anticipate those of Crabbe more than a century later. Dryden's stories, mainly translations or adaptations, are all in heroic couplets. One may say about these *Fables* what he himself remarked about *The Canterbury Tales:* "There is such a variety of game springing up before me, that I am distracted in my choice, and know not which to follow. 'Tis sufficient to say according to the proverb, that here is God's plenty." Of this God's plenty we have space for only a brief examination of one of Dryden's best-managed narratives, the story of "Theodore and Honoria" from Boccaccio.

This poem of 428 lines is a melodramatic tale of terror, in which the skilfully controlled technique and tempo of the verse sustain and unify the whole narrative. Structurally the poem is divided into four parts, the first and last relatively short (71 and 49 lines) and the central two considerably longer (145 and 163 lines). The opening part rapidly sketches in the essential exposition: the setting and Theodore's fixed but unrequited passion for Honoria. Part II presents the atmosphere and action of the grisly scene from hell, in which Theodore sees his ghostly ancestor pursue and kill an equally ghostly woman for whom he died of love and whom he is now fated to avenge in this manner. Part III gives us Theodore's elaborate plan to reveal this terrifying pursuit and vengeance to Honoria and her family. Part IV is the conclusion, in which Honoria, profiting by the experience, has a change of heart and marries Theodore.

Except in the thirty triplets scattered throughout the poem, full enjambment occurs rarely as a device to knit the couplets together and speed them up. The most extreme instance appears in the following six lines:

> "As many months as I sustained her hate,
> So many years is she condemned by Fate
> To daily death; and every several place
> Conscious of her disdain and my disgrace,
> Must witness her just punishment, and be
> A scene of triumph and revenge to me." (199-204)

For the most part the couplets are firmly end-stopped, the syntactic structures parallel rather than oblique. Balance and antithesis, as well as other technical characteristics of the verse form, appear in the following passage:

> Nor prayers nor tears nor offered vows could move;
> The work went backward; and the more he strove
> To advance his suit, the farther from her love.

Wearied at length, and wanting remedy,
He doubted oft, and oft resolved to die.
But pride stood ready to prevent the blow,
For who would die to gratify a foe?
His generous mind disdained so mean a fate;
That passed, his next endeavour was to hate.
But vainer that relief than all the rest;
The less he hoped, with more desire possessed;
Love stood the siege, and would not yield his breast.

(22-33)

In the second and third lines, note the parallelism of "the more" and "the farther" and the antithesis of "went backward" and "To advance." In line 5, however, the near-parallel of the constructions "doubted oft" and "oft resolved" is partially unbalanced by the inversion of the second in terms of the first. In the next couplet there is a strong thought contrast between "generous mind," on the one hand, and both "so mean a fate" and "to hate" on the other. Finally, we may note balance and contrast in the next to the last line: "The less he hoped" and "with more desire." Throughout the passage the tempo varies interestingly from unit to unit, as, for example, the slowness of the opening triplet in contrast to the speed of the couplet which follows. Alliteration is also marked in lines 4, 5, 6, 7, 8, and 12.

The creation of atmosphere is powerfully aided by the music and cadence of the couplets, which reflect the ominous tones of nature itself:

While listening to the murmuring leaves he stood
More than a mile immersed within the wood,
At once the wind was laid; the whispering sound
Was dumb; a rising earthquake rocked the ground;
With deeper brown the grove was overspread,
A sudden horror seized his giddy head,
And his ears tinkled, and his colour fled.
Nature was in alarm; some danger nigh

Seemed threatened, though unseen to mortal eye.
Unused to fear, he summoned all his soul,
And stood collected in himself, and whole;
Not long; for soon a whirlwind rose around,
And from afar he heard a screaming sound,
As of a dame distressed, who cried for aid,
And filled with loud laments the secret shade.   (88-102)

The identification of the man and nature reinforces the iden-
tical mood of both—a mood of terror and suspense. To
this total effect the alliteration which plays over the entire
passage contributes, as do the almost equal variation between
four- and five-stress lines and the movement of the caesura
from the second syllable at one extreme to the eighth at the
other.

With the characters introduced and the atmosphere cre-
ated, Dryden carries the story forward swiftly and without
interruption. The heroic verse becomes the medium for pure
narration, of which the following lines are typical:

Well pleased were all his friends, the task was light,
The father, mother, daughter they invite;
Hardly the dame was drawn to this repast;
But yet resolved, because it was the last.
The day was come, the guests invited came,
And with the rest the inexorable dame:
A feast prepared with riotous expense,
Much cost, more care, and most magnificence.
The place ordained was in that haunted grove
Where the revenging ghost pursued his love.   (247-56)

For unadorned directness and clarity these couplets would
be difficult to surpass. They set and maintain a fast narra-
tive pace, because of the predominence of four-stress lines
and the use of polysyllabic words and a simple straight-
forward syntax. Only one line (line 8) is more descriptive
than narrative, and that line is strikingly balanced and allit-
erative. Finally, the weight and importance of the rhymes

give the whole passage a ringing quality and justify the observation that "Dryden at his best did not smother his rhymes, but propelled himself by them and by the steady forward stroke of the end-stopped couplet."[15]

The "energy divine," a marked characteristic of Dryden's best narratives, is an even more important ingredient in his lyrics in heroic verse. His best known lyrical poems—the irregular Pindarics, *Alexander's Feast* and *Mrs. Anne Killigrew*—are not in this form. Yet of all the masters of the heroic couplet, Dryden was most successful in adapting the form to the meter of song. His best odes and songs in heroic verse deserve to be better known, for in quality they surpass the more familiar anthology pieces.

One of Dryden's methods of making the heroic couplet sing was to fix the caesura at the end of the third metrical foot and employ feminine or other two-syllable rhymes almost exclusively. These effects appear most often in the songs from the plays, of which the following from *The Maiden Queen* is typical:

> I feed a flame within, which so torments me,
> That it both pains my heart, and yet contents me;
> 'Tis such a pleasing smart, and I so love it,
> That I had rather die than once remove it.
>
> Yet he for whom I grieve shall never know it;
> My tongue does not betray, nor my eyes show it:
> Not a sigh, nor a tear, my pain discloses,
> But they fall silently, like dew on roses.
>
> Thus to prevent my love from being cruel,
> My heart's the sacrifice, as 'tis the fuel;
> And while I suffer this, to give him quiet
> My faith rewards my love, though he deny it.
>
> On his eyes will I gaze, and there delight me;
> Where I conceal my love, no frown can fright me;
> To be more happy, I dare not aspire;
> Nor can I fall more low, mounting no higher.

[15] Van Doren, *op. cit.*, p. 219.

The movement of these lines is fast and energetic, and the extra-syllable rhymes give an upward lilt at the end of each line. With one exception (line 15), the medial pause occurs after the sixth syllable, which further disguises the "heroic" quality of the couplet by tending to divide each line into threes and twos. In addition, the whole poem is varied by the more-than-usual amount of anapestic substitution. This is not a good poem, and indeed it may be questioned whether in lines 6, 7, 13, and 15 the iambic norm is not strained too severely by the prominence of this variation. However that may be, the anapests do contribute a lyrical movement with a vengeance! Another song from another one of the plays, which has been analyzed by Yvor Winters,[16] illustrates similar lyrical qualities, with the addition of the use of internal rhyme.

Van Doren has observed that "Dryden was a born writer of hymns, though the hymns he wrote were seldom labelled as such. Praise with him was as instinctive as satire; he delighted as much in glorious openings and surging, up-gathered invocations as in contemptuous 'characters.' "[17] One hymn, the translation "Te Deum" (the authorship of which has been questioned), is so labelled, and it does contain Dryden's characteristic lyrical harmonies:

> Both heaven and earth thy majesty display;
> They owe their beauty to thy glorious ray.
> Thy praises fill the loud apostles' quire:
> The train of prophets in the song conspire.
> Legions of Martyrs in the chorus shine,
> And vocal blood with vocal music join.   (10-15)

Here the caesura varies between the fourth and fifth syllable, and the lines are predominantly four-stress, with either the third or the fourth accent suppressed. The suppression of

---

[16] *Op. sit.*, pp. 135-36; the song is "No, no, poor suff'ring heart, no change endeavour," from *Cleomenes, the Spartan Hero* (1692).

[17] *Op. cit.*, p. 192.

the stress at these points adds a quickened movement to the
second half of each line by substituting a pyrrhic foot for the
expected iambic.

Despite the reputation of that magnificent *tour de force*,
Alexander's Feast, and the many exquisite songs in the plays
and lyrical passages in the other poems (including the im-
pressive opening of *Religio Laici*), Dryden's most success-
ful lyric *in toto* is the elegy *To the Memory of Mr. Oldham*.
Because it is less well known than it deserves, I shall quote
it in full:

> Farewell, too little and too lately known,
> Whom I began to think and call my own:
> For sure our souls were near allied, and thine
> Cast in the same poetic mould with mine.
> One common note on either lyre did strike,
> And knaves and fools we both abhorred alike.
> To the same goal did both our studies drive:
> The last set out the soonest did arrive.
> Thus Nisus fell upon the slippery place,
> Whilst his young friend performed and won the race.
> O early ripe! to thy abundant store
> What could advancing age have added more?
> It might (what nature never gives the young)
> Have taught the numbers of thy native tongue.
> But satire needs not those, and wit will shine
> Through the harsh cadence of a rugged line.
> A noble errour, and but seldom made,
> When poets are by too much force betrayed.
> Thy generous fruits, though gathered ere their prime,
> Still showed a quickness; and maturing time
> But mellows what we write to the dull sweets of rhyme.
> Once more, hail, and farewell! farewell, thou young,
> But ah! too short, Marcellus of our tongue!
> Thy brows with ivy and with laurels bound;
> But fate and gloomy night encompass thee around.

In structure as well as lyrical movement this poem is superbly written. Logically the couplets are unified into two main parts and a short conclusion: the first ten, the second eleven, and the last four lines. The opening exclamation of the second part (line 11) includes in its meaning the idea of the first line of the poem, thus knitting the parts more closely together. The first line of the conclusion (line 22) practically repeats this first line, which gives the poem a compact circular structure. Finally, the element of suspense is maintained by not resolving the hint of death in the first line until the very end: "But fate and gloomy night encompass thee around."

The accompanying emotional meanings are no less precise and powerful. Each of the three parts, for example, is introduced with a strong lyrical note, in which the music echoes and reinforces the feeling: "Farewell, too little and too lately known . . . O early ripe! . . . Once more, hail, and farewell!" The one triplet comes at a crucial and climactic point (just before the short conclusion), and by expressing the most powerful emotion thus far, prepares for the exclamations that follow. Individual lines and groups of lines, by themselves and in context, also denote a wide variety of strong but modulated feeling—for example, lines 3-4, 6, 12, 15-16, and 19-22. In structure, in execution within the structure, and as lyric poetry, this elegy merits the praise which T. S. Eliot has given it: "From the perfection of such an elegy we cannot detract; the lack of nebula is compensated by the satisfying completeness of the statement."[18]

There can be no doubt that Dryden's best heroic couplets, as well as his best poetry, appear in the dozens of "occasional" poems that he wrote. These are all expository, ratiocinative, or, in the best sense, didactic; and they include the satires, prologues, epilogues, and epistles. The reasons for Dryden's excelling in this kind of poetry have been set forth by Van

[18] *Homage to John Dryden*, p. 23.

Doren and Eliot.[19]   Dryden is a poet of magnificent denotation; his mastery of rhetorical language rivals that of Milton; and his mastery of range, energy, and music in verse is equally great.

The quality of magniloquence arises frequently in the satires, but it is most prominent in Part I of *Absalom and Achitophel*, in which the epic-like structure, the mock-heroic style, and the Miltonic influence give scope for some of Dryden's most characteristic effects:

> What cannot praise effect in mighty minds,
> When flattery soothes and when ambition blinds?
> Desire of power, on earth a vicious weed,
> Yet sprung from high is of celestial seed;
> In God 'tis glory, and when men aspire,
> 'Tis but a spark too much of heavenly fire.
> The ambitious youth, too covetous of fame,
> Too full of angel's metal in his frame,
> Unwarily was led from virtue's ways,
> Made drunk with honour and debauched with praise.

(303-12)

The tone of this passage is heroic and rhetorical—the result of a complex combination of vowel and consonant music (with pronounced alliteration), crisply varied movement (accentuated by polysyllables), and meaning (weighty and abstract: the desire for power).   For Dryden the placement of the caesura is relatively regular: with one exception (line 8) it occurs near the middle of the line after the fourth, fifth, or sixth syllable.   The number of stresses per line varies between four and five.   This regularity adds to the tone of dignity.   The couplets are end-stopped, except for the last two, which, although not fully enjambed, are syntactically united by having the subject ("The ambitious youth") in the first and the complement ("Unwarily was led") in the second.

[19] See, for example, Van Doren, *op. cit.*, p. 71; and Eliot, *Homage to John Dryden*, pp. 16 and 18.

Credit for the triumph of the heroic couplet in satire must be divided between Dryden and Pope, and so much has been written about their satires that to add another word may seem an act of supererogation. But one characteristic has been generally overlooked, that of dramatic tension. Because of the presence of tensions on the various levels of rhythm, sound, syntax, and meaning, good neo-classic satire is not one-sided nor too exclusively satiric.

Part I of *Absalom and Achitophel*, for example, is not merely a satire. Within it, almost equally emphasized, are the contrasting attitudes of approval and disapproval; and between these extremities the rhythm, sound, syntax, and meaning shuttle back and forth to create an intricate complex of patterns. Indicative of the dramatic tension thus created are the relationships among the four major portraits evenly spaced throughout the poem, those of Monmouth, Shaftesbury, Buckingham, and Ormond ("Absalom," "Achitophel," "Zimri," and "Barzillai"). In terms of contrasting attitudes, the portraits are exactly balanced, two (Monmouth and Ormond) being sympathetic and two (Shaftesbury and Buckingham) being satiric. Of the other full-length portraits, the two most important (Slingsby Bethel as "Shimei" and Titus Oates as "Corah") are satiric; but they are counterbalanced by the sympathetic pictures of Rochester as "Hushai" and Edward Seymour as "Amiel." In addition, there are two groups of smaller fry, set off in thumbnail sketches against each other—the malcontents and the loyalists. Finally, Shaftesbury's speeches as an evil force stand in contrast to Charles II's concluding speech as a power for good.

Within the portraits themselves tensions are set up in various ways. Thus in the following body–soul contrast, the verbs "fretted" and "o'er-informed" create under pressure a union of the opposites:

> A fiery soul, which, working out its way,
> Fretted the pigmy body to decay,
> And o'er-informed the tenement of clay. (156-58)

In the opening lines on Buckingham, at least two readings are possible, both having the same destructive effect and illustrating a kind of intentional ambiguity:

> A man so various that he seemed to be
> Not one, but all mankind's epitome:
> Stiff in opinions, always in the wrong;
> Was everything by starts and nothing long. (545-48)

The tension arises from the complete and unexpected reversal of meaning between the two couplets. The first may be interpreted as a serious sympathetic tribute; the second is, of course, devastating satire. According to this reading, the first couplet is a build-up for the purpose of enhancing the letdown that follows. Another interpretation would make the first couplet pure irony, so that the meaning of both couplets is the same, yet the surface meaning of the first remains in opposition to that of the second.

The element of surprise, often involving conflict, also appears within individual lines of the poem. The following passage is a case in point:

> Shimei, whose youth did early promise bring
> Of zeal to God and hatred to his king,
> Did wisely from expensive sins refrain,
> And never broke the Sabbath, but for gain. (585-88)

In the first couplet "early promise" leads the reader to expect something admirable; that expectation is realized in "zeal to God," but the remainder of the line gives him an unexpected shock. Similarly in the second couplet the complimentary "And never broke the Sabbath" is blasted by the stinging satire of "but for gain." This texture of opposites is further complicated and intensified by the irony of the preceding line, which is concentrated in the word "wisely" as applied to sin. Tensions created by this inversion of expected meanings are numerous in Dryden. Thus of Buckingham he says:

> In squandering wealth was his peculiar art;
> Nothing went unrewarded but desert.   (559-60)

A more famous example appears in *MacFlecknoe:*

> The rest to some faint meaning make pretense,
> But Shadwell never deviates into sense.   (19-20)

In *Absalom and Achitophel* the music and the tempo of the poetry also create tensions which reinforce the dramatic conflicts of meaning. Note, for instance, the contrast in length of vowels and speed of movement between the lines of the following couplet:

> A fiery soul, which, working out its way,
> Fretted the pigmy body to decay . . .

The first line is slow and weighty; the second, fast and explosive. Similarly about Buckingham:

> Beggared by fools, whom still he found too late,
> He had his jest, and they had his estate.   (561-62)

And note what alliteration does to the meaning of the following passage:

> For close designs, and crooked counsels fit;
> Sagacious, bold, and turbulent of wit;
> Restless, unfixed in principles and place;
> In power unpleased, impatient of disgrace.   (152-55)

The explosive *k* and *p* sounds intensify the feeling of distaste and disfavor; the hissing *s* sounds further reinforce this idea, which thus builds up an attitude of supreme contempt. All of this interplay of thought, feeling, music, and movement adds enormously to the total effect of the poem.

Second only to the satires in richness, variety, and excellence, Dryden's prologues and epilogues form a compact body of splendid heroic verse. These poems deal with almost every subject under the sun, but Van Doren has divided them roughly into nine groups.[20] The quality, if not the variety, of Dryden's achievement in this kind of occasional poem can be indicated by brief samplings from the ninety-five that he is known to have written. One of the more typical is his Prologue to *All for Love*, on the subject of critics.

Structurally this poem is divided into three parts: the first eighteen, the next twelve, and the last ten lines. Part I opens with a triplet announcing the main subject:

> What flocks of critics hover here today,
> As vultures wait on armies for their prey,
> All gaping for the carcase of a play!

The identification of critics with vultures in the second line is prepared for by the use of "flocks" in the first. This identification is continued in the following couplet by reference to the "croaking notes" of the critics. Next, the author ironically gives himself up, after which he introduces the subject of his play, the story of Antony and Cleopatra. Part I ends with another triplet:

> I could name more; a wife, and mistress too,
> Both (to be plain) too good for most of you;
> The wife well-natured, and the mistress true.   (16-18)

The note of author-audience intimacy, characteristic of all the prologues and epilogues, appears in the second line above. So far as the subject under discussion is concerned, this second line could be omitted; but it is vital to the Prologue for its dramatic effect as an "aside." Part II continues the theme of critics by giving them advice and attacking witless critics

[20] As follows: (1) "those which celebrate theatrical occasions," (2) "those which compliment distinguished spectators or flatter special audiences," (3) "those which deal in literary criticism," (4) "those which introduce young playwrights," (5) "those which berate the audience for its low taste," (6) "those which play with contemporary manners," (7) "those which seem to have been calculated to please through sheer brutal innuendo," (8) "the political prologues and epilogues," and (9) "those which are personal or controversial": *op. cit.*, pp. 134-46.

and fops. Near the center of the passage Dryden drives his
point home in an epigrammatic couplet:

> Errors, like straws, upon the surface flow;
> He who would search for pearls must dive below. (25-26)

Part III turns to compliment and ends with ironic under-
statement about the poet's play:

> And since that plenteous autumn now is past,
> Whose grapes and peaches have indulged your taste,
> Take in good part from our poor poet's board
> Such rivelled fruits as winter can afford.

All the lines of this Prologue move with that smooth,
sure touch that a little later was to become the hallmark of
Dryden's art. The first three, for example, illustrate a
sharply increasing tempo. The first is a normal pentameter,
with five stresses; the second is four-stress, with the fourth
accent suppressed; the third, with two expected accents sup-
pressed because they fall on prepositions ("for" and "of"),
is a fast-moving three-stress line. The couplets suggest the
tones of a speaking voice (as in a good prologue they should),
yet they create an atmosphere of dignified informality, which
is the great characteristic of the Dryden prologue.

A more condensed and unified poem is the Epilogue
to *The Conquet of Granada,* Part II. The subject is liter-
ary criticism, which here takes the form of a detailed contrast
between Jonsonian and Restoration drama. In structure the
poem is evenly divided between these two themes. A touch
of sardonic humor appears in the couplet on the reputation of
the "giants before the flood":

> Fame then was cheap, and the first comer sped;
> And they have kept it since, by being dead.

In its sharp unexpectedness, the last phrase anticipates the
brittle wit of the later satires. But most distinctive in this
poem is the precision and economy with which the couplets

express infinite riches in a little room. Note, for instance, the clarity, smoothness, and tight logic of the following passage:

> Wit's now arrived to a more high degree;
> Our native language more refined and free;
> Our ladies and our men now speak more wit
> In conversation, than those poets writ.
> Then, one of these, is consequently true;
> That what this poet writes comes short of you
> And imitates you ill (which most he fears),
> Or else his writing is not worse than theirs.   (23-30)

Technically this is the mature Dryden couplet; in his hands it has become "a strong yet light vehicle for miscellaneous loads, a medium for the poetry of statement."[21]

III

Even more so than Dryden, Pope has been a martyr to a cause. As the arch-priest of the heroic couplet, he has become the personification of the form at its best and worst. He was personally the kind of man to invite this identification, and the nineteenth-century critics made the most of it! But within certain limits Pope's achievements were so superlative that the final norm of the heroic couplet must be based upon his work. The norm has been described and analyzed by many critics, especially Root and Tillotson.[22]

Dryden, as we have seen, uses the couplet for numerous purposes, varying it to suit these ends. "Pope, in combining a comparable diversity into a single complexity, varies the couplet noticeably less than does Dryden; yet . . . to the reader familiar with his sensibility he is one of the most exquisitely finished, as well as one of the most profoundly moving, poets in English."[23] Pope's work may conveniently be divided into four groups: the pastorals, the translations, the didactic-reflective poems, and the satires. At his best in

[21] Van Doren, *op. cit.*, p. 76.
[22] See Root, *op. cit.*, pp. 32-50; and Tillotson, *op. cit.*, pp. 105-40.
[23] Winters, *op. cit.*, p. 138.

these relatively limited fields, Pope concentrated "diversity into a single complexity" that revealed the heroic couplet to perfection. After him the masters of this form achieved distinction by exploiting the various aspects of it in which he (and, less directly, Dryden) had shown the way.

Rightly understood, the "cool pastorals," which Pope wrote at an early age, become exquisite poems in a tradition that required them to be just as they are. Like Shakespeare's first three comedies, the pastorals are apprentice work and are, in the best sense, "imitations" of the classical pastoral, particularly Virgil's. The couplets are apprentice work mainly in their lack of flexibility: they are chiselled and polished to perfection, but in them Pope has not yet learned to "snatch a grace beyond the reach of art." Thus, in the following couplets from the pastoral *Summer:*

> For you the swains the fairest flowers design,
> And in one garland all their beauties join;
> Accept the wreath which you deserve alone,
> In whom all beauties are comprised in one.   (55-58)

The first three lines have the normal five stresses, but in the fourth line the medial accent is suppressed. All metrical feet are iambic except the first two in the second, and the third in the fourth, line. The caesura alternately follows the fourth and fifth syllables (4-5-4-5), and alliteration is marked throughout the passage. In terms of the thought, the two couplets are united by the relationship between the second and fourth lines: "in one garland all their beauties join . . . In whom all beauties are comprised in one."

The famous lines from this pastoral, the last four lines of which were set to music by Handel, are also relatively inflexible, but they reveal, to a marked degree, the characteristic parallel syntax of heroic verse:

> O deign to visit our forsaken seats,
> The mossy fountains, and the green retreats!

Where'er you walk, cool gales shall fan the glade,
Trees, where you sit, shall crowd into a shade:
Where'er you tread, the blushing flowers shall rise,
And all things flourish where you turn your eyes. (71-76)

The second and third couplets are made parallel by the repetition of the two "where'er" and the two "where" constructions. The former introduce both couplets and are, therefore, identical in structure. But the two "where's," although generally parallel, are not identically so, because of the variation in word order. To be exactly parallel, the last line would have to read: "And all things, where you turn your eyes, flourish."

Windsor Forest is closely linked to the earlier pastorals, particularly if we consider it as two separate poems rather crudely joined. The first part (the first 290 lines and a six-line conclusion transplanted, with variations, to the end of the standard version) is a pastoral poem. It is noteworthy on two counts. First, in structure and subject matter it is closer to certain poems by Waller and Denham than to the classical pastoral; second, the couplets reveal technical improvements over those of Pope's earlier pastorals. After the traditional appeal to the muses, Pope echoes the opening lines of Waller's "On St. James's Park" in the following couplets:

The groves of Eden, vanished now so long,
Live in description, and look green in song:
These, were my breast inspired with equal flame,
Like them in beauty, should be like in fame. (7-10)

Waller's poem begins:

Of the first Paradise there's nothing found;
Plants set by Heaven are vanished, and the ground;
Yet the description lasts; who knows the fate
Of lines that shall this paradise relate?
Instead of rivers rolling by the side
Of Eden's garden, here flows in the tide.

The structural and technical superiority of Pope over Waller is manifest. The music and the movement of the second passage are awkward and bumpy; the second line is especially inept, with its afterthought "and the ground" tacked on for the sake of the rhyme. In contrast, Pope's first couplet is impressively well modulated, and all four lines reveal the hand of a master.

In theme and structure the first part of *Windsor Forest* is modelled on Denham's *Cooper's Hill*, to which Pope pays high tribute (lines 271 and 280). Both are descriptive-meditative poems, with the description dominant in Pope, the meditation in Denham. As Root has shown, the shorter *Windsor Forest* possesses a firm structural unity,[24] which is superior to that of *Cooper's Hill*. Like Denham Pope introduces descriptions of the variety of fish, animal, and bird life in Windsor Forest; but in *Cooper's Hill* these take the form of the eighty-four-line account of a stag hunt, which is so overlong that it gravely weakens the unity of the whole poem.

The relative inflexibility of the couplets in the earlier pastorals is considerably modified in *Windsor Forest*. In this poem there are far more deviations from the fixed norm of the early Pope couplet, particularly a greater elasticity of movement:

> Here hills and vales, the woodland and the plain,
> Here earth and water seem to strive again;
> Not chaos-like together crushed and bruised,
> But, as the world, harmoniously confused:
> Where order in variety we see,
> And where, though all things differ, all agree. (11-16)

Increased variety appears in the number of stresses and the placement of the caesura in this passage. Although the other lines contain four or five stresses, line 5 is unexpectedly three-

[24] *Op. cit.*, pp. 65-67.

stress. The first four lines have caesuras regularly after the fourth or fifth syllables, but line 5 is again an exception, having no caesura; and in the last line the caesura occurs either after the second or the seventh syllable. The number and the arrangement of polysyllabic words add to the flexibility of movement; and finally, although the couplets are all end-stopped, syntactic balance and antithesis unite them into a group.

In translation, as in other things, Pope's interests were not so varied as Dryden's; but the famous Englishing of *The Iliad* has eclipsed all other verse translations of the classical epic, including Dryden's *Aeneid*. Pope's *Iliad* may not have been Homer, as Dr. Bentley said (what translation is?), but it became a model for the heroic couplet and yet, regrettably, the storehouse of an elegant language which, in the hands of imitators, degenerated into "poetic diction." For our purposes, these considerations are less important than the fact that Pope's work on *The Iliad* and *The Odyssey* occupies a place in his development of the couplet similar to that of the heroic plays in Dryden's career. Both the translations and the dramas were elaborate proving grounds for the final perfection of the heroic couplet. By 1717, when Lintot published his collected *Works* in folio, Pope was in the midst of his struggles with *The Iliad*, the first volume of which had appeared two years before. This task was completed in 1720—all "19,000 well-turned lines."

It is in the didactic poems (including the satires) that we find Pope's most mature and greatest work. To appreciate him at his best, and indeed to appreciate the whole neo-classic tradition before and after him, requires a preliminary consideration of the word "didactic," because unfortunately it has become a term of reproach in the modern critical vocabulary. The supposed "revolt" against neo-classic theory and practice first made an issue of didacticism in the early nineteenth century. Since then the critical attacks from Hazlitt to John Crowe Ransom today have left didactic poetry almost defenseless. Root has deplored this situation in his evaluation of Pope's "moralized song," as have a few other modern critics, notably Eliot, Winters, and Van Doren.[25]

The two characteristics most often associated with didacticism in poetry are a moral purpose and a generalized vocabulary. Pope's famous assertion that "The proper study of Mankind is Man" implies one of the functions of all good poetry: the interpretation of man's nature to himself. To this ethical function classical criticism joined the esthetic function of giving pleasure, which Pope and his contemporaries considered the more important of the two. The balance between these Horatian principles is described by Boileau in his influential *Art Poétique:*

> Qu'en savantes leçons votre muse fertile,
> Partout joigne au plaisant le solide et l'utile.
> Un lecteur sage fuit un vain amusement,
> Et veut mettre à profit son divertissement.

(IV, 87-90)

The following incisive paragraph elaborates on Boileau's generalizations:

The specifically didactic poem, such as the *Essay on Man,* does not merely suggest instruction; it begins . . . with an abstract proposition, a philosophical thesis. It is in its inception a poetry of intellectual ideas rather than of sensations and emotions. Such is the raw material thrown into the crucible of poetic creation. In the poetry which emerges the intellectual idea is still present, but it is now transfigured: what was a thesis has become an image; the abstract has taken on concretion; what was dead and inert now glows incandescent with poetic fire; what was somewhat baldly prose has taken on the rhythm and texture of an exquisitely modulated verse.[26]

[25] Eliot, *Homage to John Dryden,* pp. 13-23; Winters, *op. cit.,* pp. 361-74; Van Doren, *op. cit., passim.*

[26] Root, *op. cit.,* p. 163.

This is indeed a far cry from the thesis that "A poem should not mean but be"!

More specifically we may consider how this combination of instruction and entertainment operates in a fourteen-line passage from the *Essay on Man:*

> Heaven from all creatures hides the book of Fate,
> All but that page prescribed their present state:
> From brutes what men, from men what spirits know:
> Or who could suffer Being here below?
> The lamb thy riot dooms to bleed today,
> Had he thy reason, would he skip and play?
> Pleased to the last, he crops the flowery food,
> And licks the hand just raised to shed his blood.
> Oh blindness to the future! kindly given,
> That each may fill the circle marked by Heaven:
> Who sees with equal eye, as God of all,
> A hero perish, or a sparrow fall,
> Atoms or systems into ruin hurled,
> And now a bubble burst, and now a world.   (I, 77-90)

The controlled magniloquence of this passage makes it something far different from its prose thesis that blindness to the future is a blessing and is necessary for the fulfillment of divine purpose. After an impressive generalization in the first four lines, the next four give a specific example of the larger thesis, an example which also deepens the emotional significance of that thesis. Then with the exclamation "Oh blindness to the future!" the remainder of the passage acquires a lyrical power that infuses the quality of a vision into the bare universality of the concluding couplets. There is deep ethical meaning, but there is also song of a very moving kind. The lyrical tone is further reinforced by the structure of the passage, which divides into the octave and sestet of a sonnet.

Even couplets and individual lines from Pope have, out of context, a quality not usually associated with didactic poetry. For example, the well-known "Die of a rose in aromatic pain," which, as Root says, might easily have come out of Keats; and the couplet praised by Tennyson:

> The spider's web, how exquisitely fine!
> Feels at each thread, and lives along the line.

But in their contexts, these and dozens of other lines in the *Moral Essays* are the imaginative demonstration of a thesis. Taken all together, they reveal one of the abiding neo-classic beliefs: "for an intelligent reader . . . the highest pleasure is that which is joined to wisdom."[27]

The second characteristic of didactic poetry concerns its language. In accordance with neo-classic theory, of which Johnson's warning against "numbering the streaks of the tulip" is the *locus classicus*, the eighteenth-century poetic vocabulary tended to be generalized and denotative. As part of the rationalistic temper of the times, this tendency helped to create the familiar neo-classic poetry of statement (rather than suggestion), in which the preference was for abstractions (often personified) and obvious (rather than recondite) imagery. For us today the contrast is sharpest in the use of imagery. Johnson's famous strictures on meta-physical poetry in the "Life of Cowley" state the case for neo-classicism: poetic imagery should deal in similarities rather than "occult resemblances in things apparently un-like."[28] Such generalized language and obvious imagery ap-pear frequently in all great poetry, ancient and modern, de-spite "the doctrinaire conviction" of many critics "that a mere abstract statement cannot be poetry."[29]

In Pope these qualities may be illustrated on almost every page of the *Moral Essays*—for instance, the following pas-sage from Epistle II "Of the Characters of Women":

[27] Root, *op. cit.*, p. 161.
[28] See R. L. Sharp, *From Donne to Dryden*, pp. 150-75.
[29] Winters, *op. cit.*, p. 531.

Pleasures the sex, as children Birds pursue,
Still out of reach, yet never out of view;
Sure, if they catch, to spoil the Toy at most,
To covet flying, and regret when lost:
At last, to follies Youth could scarce defend,
It grows their Age's prudence to pretend;
Ashamed to own they gave delight before,
Reduced to feign it, when they give no more:
As Hags hold Sabbaths, less for joy than spite,
So these their merry, miserable Night;
Still round and round the Ghosts of Beauty glide,
And haunt the places where their Honour died.

                                        (231-42)

"Pleasures," "follies," "prudence," "delight"—the whole
passage is built upon abstract ideas; and personification occurs
often: "Youth," "Age," "Night," "Ghosts of Beauty," "Hon-
our." Two images are used, the first one rather elaborate
for Pope. It is worked out in the first four lines: women
pursue pleasure as children pursue birds. The second occurs
in the ninth and tenth lines: as hags keep the Sabbath out of
spite, so women grown old maintain "their merry, miserable
Night." The elements of similarity in these comparisons
far outweigh their unlikenesses; the focal points of the images
are therefore relatively close together. The entire passage
illustrates one of Pope's great achievements: "the statement
in language at once general, concentrated, dignified, and
pathetic of a truth both tragic and so universal as to be wholly.
impersonal."[30]

The intricate and fascinating details of Pope's masterful
accomplishments in satire would be out of place in this intro-
duction to the work of his followers. Besides, as with Dry-
den's satire, they have been adequately dealt with else-
where.[31] It should be noted, however, that, like Dryden's,

[30] Winters, op. cit., p. 136.
[31] See Root, op. cit., pp. 187-227; Tillotson, op. cit., passim; Leavis, op. cit.,
pp. 68-101; and Nicoll Smith, op. cit., pp. 9-31.

Pope's satire as poetry is not too narrowly satiric. It too makes use of dramatic tension to expand its full significance into the realm of great poetry. Although even the early and mildly satiric *Rape of the Lock* illustrates this point, the mature *Epistle to Dr. Arbuthnot* drives it home.

This poem may be divided into sections of "attack" and sections of "defense," which at their extremes represent the satiric versus the sympathetic attitudes. There are roughly three sections of attack and three of defense, which alternate throughout the poem. The first section (lines 1-124) is an attack on the pseudo-poets who are annoying Pope; the second section (125-92) is Pope's defense against them; the third section (193-214) is the famous attack on Atticus; the fourth (215-304) is another defense; the fifth (305-34) is the attack upon Sporus; and the last is a third defense leading to the conclusion of the poem.

Thus simplified and abstracted from the poem, the two groups of sections appear to have little in common except their mutual exclusiveness. Actually, however, they rarely present either single isolated extreme. Usually between and within sections, subsections, couplets, and even lines occurs an infinite variety of fluctuations, which sets up the tensions that make the poem. Lines 3 and 4 illustrate in miniature this pattern of tensions:

> The Dog-star rages! nay, 'tis past a doubt,
> All Bedlam, or Parnassus, is let out . . .

The key words are "Bedlam" and "Parnassus"; the first is a home for the insane, the second the mythological home of the poets. The conjunction "or" equates insane people with poets; but Pope and many of his friends knew themselves to be poets who are certainly not being disparaged here. In context, therefore, the full meaning of "Parnassus" includes an intentional contradiction: the word is used both ironically and sympathetically to point out the distinction between pseudo-poets and true poets. Similarly the seeming paradox of the couplet,

> He, who still wanting, tho' he lives on theft,
> Steals much, spends little, yet has nothing left,

is fully resolved in its context (lines 179-90).

Another kind of intricate thought pattern involving tensions occurs in the transition from the satire against Bufo to the praise to Pope's friend Gay. First about Bufo:

> But still the *Great* have kindness in reserve,
> He helped to bury whom he helped to starve. (247-48)

Next the couplet introducing the praise of Gay:

> Blessed be the *Great!* for those they take away,
> And those they left me; for they left me Gay. (255-56)

These couplets are only six lines apart, so the reader should have the first in mind when he comes to the second. The key to both in context is the word "Great." The line in which this word first appears is pure irony, for it climaxes the attack on Bufo. The second one, however, is a mixture of satire and approval: the Great are complimented ironically for relieving Pope of the fools ("those they take away"), and at the same time they are sincerely complimented for leaving him Gay, who is one of "those they left me." A final and more subtle complication arises from the suggestion that the Great are also fools themselves for not appreciating a man like Gay.

Even in the brilliantly satiric portrait of Atticus, all is by no means satire. Both the opening lines and the concluding one are complimentary and sympathetic, thus forming a frame within which the controlled satire operates:

> Peace to all such! but were there one whose fires
> True Genius kindles, and fair fame inspires;

> Blest with each talent and each art to please,
> And born to write, converse, and live with ease:
>
> .   .   .   .   .   .
>
> Who would not weep, if Atticus were he?   (193-214)

This framework of compliment enclosing an area of attack intensifies both attitudes and achieves a union of opposites. And, unlike the opening of Dryden's portrait of Buckingham, there is no reason to read the above lines as irony. Conversely, in one of the sections of defense (lines 215-304), where Pope is picturing himself sympathetically, appears the passage of attack on Bufo, who is introduced to heighten by contrast the rightness of Pope's position:

> I ne'er with wits or witlings passed my days,
> To spread about the itch of verse and praise;
>
> .   .   .   .   .   .
>
> But sick of fops, and poetry, and prate,
> To Bufo left the whole Castalian state.   (223-30)

In this poem the music and movement of the poetry also make their contribution to the patterns of dramatic tension. Consider, for instance, the contrast in tempo between the lines of the following couplet:

> With lenient arts extend a Mother's breath,
> Make languor smile, and smooth the bed of Death.
>
> (410-11)

the first sharp and incisive, the second slow and languorous. In another couplet there is a similar contrast, with the additional difference of five stresses in the first and only four in the second line:

> Abuse on all he loved, or loved him, spread,
> A friend in exile, or a father dead.   (354-55)

Often alliteration is used to slow up the movement, as in the following line, which also contrasts with its successor: Atticus is one whose fires,

> True Genius kindles, and fair fame inspires,
> Blest with each talent and each art to please . . .

And, of course, alliteration strengthens the tone of measured contempt in such lines as the famous,

> Damn with faint praise, assent with civil leer,
> And without sneering, teach the rest to sneer.

The whole of the *Epistle to Dr. Arbuthnot* gains immeasurably by the presence of these patterns of dramatic tension.

Other poems of Pope's, particularly *The Rape of the Lock*, possess this characteristic to a striking degree. *The Rape of the Lock* is double-edged: the tone of satire intermingles with and often itself produces a contrasting tone of sympathy for the objects satirized.[32] The poet secures a unity of sensibility by setting up dramatically opposed attitudes, between which the thought and feeling are made to fluctuate constantly.

IV

This introduction to the later masters of the heroic couplet has been intentionally eclectic, because the vast amount of work already done on Pope, Dryden, and their predecessors makes further detailed interpretation unnecessary. I have, however, tried to suggest a line of development that may be briefly described as follows. The neo-classic or heroic couplet has been written sporadically from the time of Chaucer. It appeared more frequently among the Elizabethans, still, however, the exception rather than the rule. The norm was there in individual couplets or in accidental collections of couplets; but until there appeared a conscious awareness of the unified group paragraph of such couplets, based upon a parallel syntax, the early heroic couplet had not been evolved. This circumstance occurred in the early

[32] See *The Rape of the Lock and Other Poems*, ed. Geoffrey Tillotson, pp. 106-24; Cleanth Brooks, *The Well Wrought Urn*, pp. 74-95; and Austin Warren, *Rage for Order*, pp. 37-51.

seventeenth century, in the couplet poems of Jonson, Sandys, and Falkland. It was consciously exploited by Waller and Denham, and became dominant and finally perfected in the work of Dryden and Pope.

An indication of the changes that had occurred between the Elizabethans and the eighteenth century may be seen in Pope's *Fourth Satire of Dr. John Donne* "versifyed." In Donne's first sixteen lines, which Pope takes twenty-three to translate freely, only one couplet is "heroic" enough for Pope to accept with little alteration. In Donne,

> As vain, as witless, and as false as they
> Which dwel in Court, for once going that way,

becomes in Pope's version:

> As vain, as idle, and as false, as they
> Who live at Court, for going once that Way!

Apart from the substitution of "idle," "who," and "live" for "witless," "which," and "dwel," the only other change shows the neo-classic concern for "keeping accent" in terms of significant meaning: Pope alters "once going" in the second line to "going once," so that the stressed syllable in "going" will coincide with an accent position in the iambic line. During the century and a quarter between the writing of Donne's satire and Pope's neo-classic version of it, the heroic couplet came fully into its own. For another century it flourished, despite increasingly powerful competition, because it continued to be written by a few poets who mastered the form instead of being mastered by it.

Chapter II

❧❧❧❧❧❧❧❧❧❧❧❧❧❧❧❧❧❧❧❧❧❧❧❧

Gay: Pope's Alter Ego

I

ALTHOUGH John Gay was actually a friend and con-temporary of Pope, as a poet he was also a follower. In his literary reputation, Gay has been less fortunate than other neo-classic writers; for, added to nineteenth-century neglect, he received little support from Johnson himself, whose "Life of Gay" is harsh and unsympathetic. Today, except for the *Fables* and the lyrics in *The Beggar's Opera*, Gay's poetry is more talked about than read; and more has been written about his life and times than about any of his work.[1] Even when he is occasionally judged as a poet, there is little agreement among qualified critics. At one extreme, for instance, F. R. Leavis brackets Gay with Parnell, and re-marks that they "are representative period figures, of very minor interest."[2] This is the more common view. But at the other extreme, Winters places Gay among the "chief masters of the heroic couplet."[3] These are, however, but passing estimates, the relative values of which will become apparent as we proceed.

Gay's handling of the heroic couplet, along with Pope's, represents the closest of all approximations to the neo-classic norm. The couplets are uniformly end-stopped, the caesura

---

[1] In, for example, Lewis Melville, *The Life and Letters of John Gay*; Phoebe F. Gay, *John Gay: His Place in the Eighteenth Century*; and William H. Irving, *John Gay, Favorite of the Wits.*

[2] *Op. cit.*, p. 110.   [3] *Op. cit.*, p. 134.

medially placed, and the stresses varied between four and
five to the line. In addition there are generally a balanced
syntax, propriety of sound and sense, and avoidance of ex-
pletives, triplets, alexandrines, and open vowels between
words. The following passage, selected at random from
Rural Sports, illustrates most of these characteristics:

> But I, who ne'er was bless'd by Fortune's hand,
> Nor brighten'd plough-shares in paternal land,
> Long in the noisie town have been immur'd,
> Respir'd its smoak, and all its cares endur'd,
> Where news and politicks divide mankind,
> And schemes of state involve th' uneasie mind;
> Faction embroils the world; and ev'ry tongue
> Is moved by flatt'ry, or with scandal hung.[4]

With the exception of the first line, the caesura occurs after
the 4th, 6th, 4th, 6th, 4th, 6th, and 5th syllables. All the
couplets are end-stopped; and five of the lines have five
stresses each (lines 1, 3, 4, 6, and 7), and three have four
stresses, with one accent suppressed. The balanced syntax is
especially prominent in the last couplet. In this entire poem
of 443 lines, there is only one triplet (lines 357-59) and no
alexandrines. Indeed, it is significant to note that the 1713
version of the poem contains four triplets, including one with
an alexandrine, all of which were omitted in the standard
version of 1720. And with respect to expletives, the earlier
version includes the following couplet:

> Friendship, for Sylvan Shades, does Courts despise,
> Where all must yield to Int'rest's dearer Ties. (19-20)

In the later version, the first line becomes: "Friendship, for
sylvan shades, the palace flies," thus omitting the expletive
"does."

Gay's achievements in the heroic couplet depend upon

---

[4] Lines 9-16; all references to Gay's writings are from *The Poetical Works
of John Gay,* ed. G. C. Faber.

the technical excellence of the couplets themselves and the
structural excellence of his best poems, in parts and as wholes.
His management of the four-, five-, and six-stress line is es-
sentially that of Pope, as described by Root.[5] As with Pope,
the four- and five-stress lines predominate, but all three types
appear in the following pair of couplets:

> Nor will I roam when summer's sultry rays
>
> Parch the dry ground, and spread with dust the ways;
>
> With whirling gusts the rapid atoms rise,
>
> Smoak o'er the pavement, and involve the skies.
>
> (*Trivia*, II, 315-18)

The third line above is strictly "normal," with five stressed
syllables in iambic order. The first is normal except for the
substitution of an initial trochaic foot. The second line is
"heavy" because it contains more than five stresses; in addi-
tion it also has a substituted initial trochaic foot. The fourth
line is "light," with one accent suppressed, and in it too
occurs initial trochaic substitution. Two other types of varia-
tion appear less often: the five-stress line with spondaic and
pyrrhic substitution, and the three-stress line with two normal
stresses suppressed; for example:

> While in thick woods the feeding partridge lies.
>
> (*Rural Sports*, II, 334)

> Benevolence her conversation guides.
>
> (*Epistle to a Lady*, 55)

At their best in Gay, these metrical variations create subtle
interplays that reveal the extreme flexibility of the heroic
couplet, as the following passage illustrates:

> Disdain not, Snow, my humble Verse to hear:

[5] *Op. cit.*, pp. 32-50.

Stick thy black Pen awhile behind thy Ear.
Whether thy Compter shine with Sums untold,
And thy wide-grasping Hand grow black with Gold:
Whether thy Mien erect, and sable Locks,
In Crowds of Brokers over-awe the *Stocks:*
Suspend the worldly Business of the Day;
And to enrich thy Mind, attend my Lay.

(*Epistle to Snow,* 1-8)

Of these eight lines, the first two are six-stress, the next three, five-stress, and the last three, four-stress. Except for lines 2 and 3 and 6 and 7, no one metrical foot appears initially twice in succession, the order being: iambic, trochaic, trochaic, pyrrhic, trochaic, iambic, iambic, pyrrhic. And those which do occur in succession are between, not within, couplets. Finally, metrical substitution (either spondaic or pyrrhic) occurs within five of the eight lines (in lines 1, 2, 4, 6, and 7).

Within the couplet, Gay's handling of consonant and vowel music, particularly in relationship to meaning, presents a more difficult, as it is a more important, problem. There is, of course, the usual variety of alliteration, assonance, and rhyme, which is characteristic of the well-modulated heroic couplet. When these devices are primarily matters of sound for its own sake, they merely enhance the enjoyment of the poetry; but when they affect its meaning strategically, their role becomes more vital and significant. It is probably true, as W. K. Wimsatt has pointed out,[6] that in poetry no phonetic effects are wholly unrelated to meaning. But there are degrees in this relationship: the impact of sound upon meaning will be greater in thought structures that tend to be parallel (as in satire) than in thought structures that tend to be oblique (as in pure narrative). For when there is a high degree of parallelism the music can oppose, as well as reinforce, the movement of the thought.

[6] *Op. cit.,* pp. 323-24.

In Gay's work these effects appear with great frequency, as, for instance, in the following couplet about fops:

> In gilded chariots while they loll at ease,
> And lazily insure a life's disease . . .
>
> (*Trivia*, I, 69-70)

Here the alliteration, the length of the vowels and consonants, and the rhyme play variously upon the meaning. The long *l* sounds and the long vowels in "while," "loll," "ease," "lazily," "insure," "life's," and "disease" combine to suggest in music and movement the idea of luxurious living. In the rhyme the meaning of the two words is contradictory, but the fact that they sound alike opposes this contradiction with similarity. And for pure onomatopoeia, the following passage probably received the warm approval of Pope:

> Here laden carts with thundring waggons meet,
> Wheels clash with wheels, and bar the narrow street;
> The lashing whip resounds, the horses strain,
> And blood in anguish bursts the swelling vein.
>
> (*Trivia*, II, 229-32)

But the most distinctive relationship between sound and meaning in Gay's poetry appears in constructions in which the rhymes participate in a thought "chiasmus." This device is peculiarly suited to the heroic couplet because of its characteristically parallel and antithetic structure. "Chiasmus" is a crossing of ideas between the lines of the couplet, in which both rhyme words are involved:

> There careless lies the rich brocade unroll'd,
> Here shines a cabinet with burnish'd gold.
>
> (*The Toilette*, 55-56)

The two lines communicate two sets of parallel ideas, which are related as follows: the brocade and the cabinet are the two subjects; the brocade is rich-looking, just as the cabinet is gold-covered; and the brocade is unrolled, just as the cabinet shines, to reveal its beauty and value. Similarly, but with variations:

Yet why should learning hope success at Court?
Why should our Patriots vertue's cause support?

(Epistle to Methuen, 39-40)

Court and Patriots (used ironically) are parallel, as are learning and virtue's cause; but support and success are in the logical relationship of cause-and-effect. Finally, consider:

Madmen alone their empty Dreams pursue,
And still believe the fleeting Vision true;

(Epistle to Snow, 34-35)

where dreams and vision are identical, true and empty are antithetical, and fleeting requires pursuit in this context.

Gay's management of syntactic balance, parallelism, and antithesis within the couplet gives further evidence of his mastery of the form. In his work, as in Pope's, the simplest structure is the balanced line, containing two adjective-noun phrases separated by a preposition or conjunction:

Thus hardy Theseus, with intrepid feet . . .

(Trivia, II, 83)

The tender mother, and the faithful wife.

(Epistle to a Lady, 68)

Such lines are usually four-stress, with the middle (third) accent suppressed. Other combinations may be similarly balanced:

He treads with caution, and he points with fear.

(Rural Sports, II, 314)

Variations of this line appear when a more important (and

hence stressed) word or phrase separates the balanced elements:

> Their silver coats reflect the dazling beams.
>
> (*Rural Sports*, I, 130)

Here they are separated by a verb, which may also appear at the beginning or end of the line:

> Spread their encampment o'er the spacious plain.
>
> (*Trivia*, II, 372)

> While softer chairs the tawdry load convey.
>
> (*Trivia*, I, 71)

Sometimes the syntactic balance is accompanied by a contrast in the thought, which increases complexity and requires of the poet greater skill. In the following lines "in Contemplation . . . in Straw," "with pleasure . . . with pain," and "low phrase . . . lofty theme" are all perfectly balanced, but the meaning in each pair is contrasting or contradictory:

> Where wrapp'd in Contemplation and in Straw . . .
>
> (*Epistle to Snow*, 42)

> We read with pleasure, though with pain we pay.
>
> (*Epistle to Lowndes*, 21)

> Nor with low phrase the lofty theme abuse.
>
> (*Epistle to Pulteney*, 22)

Also in the last two lines the alliterated *p* and *l* sounds re-emphasize the balanced elements and further bind them together.

Because these example are in perfect balance or contrast, the reader's expectations are always satisfied. In other instances, however, Gay (again like Pope) introduces elements that are out of balance or makes the balance one between unequal parts. The effect of this is subtle surprise—an unexpected development in structure. In the following line, the word order is unbalanced:

Endu'd by instinct, or by reason taught;
> (*Trivia*, I, 150)

for the first half leads us to expect the construction "taught by reason" instead of the inversion which the poet gives us. Similarly in the line,

> Stream eyes no more, no more thy tresses rend,
> (*Elegy on a Lap-Dog*, 20)

the second "no more" is unexpectedly inverted, as is "we pay" in the otherwise balanced line quoted above: "We read with pleasure, though with pain we pay"; and the second half of the following line:

> They love the science, and the painter prize.
> (*Epistle to Methuen*, 52)

When the balance is between two unequal parts, our attention is naturally attracted to the word or phrase that makes them unequal. I have italicized these elements in the following lines:

> And mingle profit with my *little* praise.
> (*Epistle to Methuen*, 46)

> Doom'd to survive thy joy and *only* care.
> (*Elegy on a Lap-Dog*, 4)

> Still sighs must rise, and *gen'rous* sorrow flow.
> (*Epistle to the Duchess of Marlborough*, 76)

> Summons the dogs, and greets the *dappled* morn.
> (*Rural Sports*, II, 367)

Another syntactic characteristic that strengthens and sharpens the heroic couplet is the frequency of action-words in one or both of the rhymes. "All through his work Pope seems to have preferred a verb for at least one of the rime-words in a couplet. This was a means of attaining a full stress for the rime."[7] It was also a means of achieving power

---

[7] Tillotson, *op. cit.*, p. 124.

and point in the couplet by placing one of the two most important parts of speech in a key position. In Gay the practice is as prominent as it is in Pope. Of the forty-nine couplets in the *Epistle to Paul Methuen* more than half (twenty-seven) contain at least one verb in the rhyme; and of the 221 couplets in *Rural Sports* 117 have rhyme verbs. Also the effect that Tillotson calls "bipartite unity instead . . . of unified duality" appears frequently in Gay. This is the syntactic practice of placing the verb at the end of the first line and its object in the second. The result is a kind of enjambment within the couplet:

> But let this tale to valiant virtue tell
> The daily perils of deserving well.
> *(Epistle to Methuen, 83-84)*

> Vex'd at the charge, I to the flames commit
> Rhymes, similies, Lords names, and ends of wit.
> *(Epistle to a Lady, 39-40)*

> Perhaps her patient temper can behold
> The rival of her love adorn'd with gold.
> *(The Toilette, 89-90)*

> Oft' have I seen a skilful angler try
> The various colours of the treach'rous fly.
> *(Rural Sports, I, 195-96)*

Not only within couplets, but in larger structural units Gay's handling of the form is noteworthy. Even in Pope, where the epigrammatic quality is most pronounced, the heroic couplet never wholly emancipates itself from its context. In Gay, as in Johnson, Churchill, Goldsmith, and Crabbe later, the full effects of the couplet appear in these larger units. At their best the couplets group themselves into verse paragraphs, unified by the interplay of thought, syntax, cadence, and music.

Repetition to create an elaborate syntactic parallel is one device that Gay uses, as the following passage illustrates:

How am I curst! (unhappy and forlorn)
With perjury, with love and rival's scorn!
False are the loose Coquet's inveigling airs,
False is the pompous grief of youthful heirs,
False is the cringing courtier's plighted word,
False are the dice when gamesters stamp the board,
False is the sprightly widow's publick tear;
Yet these to *Damon's* oaths are all sincere.

(*The Toilette*, 71-78)

Here the structure is obvious and mechanical. More subtle and impressive is Gay's use of parenthesis to secure the effect of enjambment between couplets without actually breaking down the pattern of the heroic couplet itself. In the following passage,

Shall he (who late *Britannia's* city trod,
And led the draggled Muse, with pattens shod,
Through dirty lanes, and alleys doubtful ways)
Refuse to write, when *Paris* asks his lays!

(*Epistle to Pulteney*, 11-14)

the two couplets could not be more indissolubly united. The main idea connects the first metrical foot of the first line with the entire last line of the second couplet: "Shall he . . . Refuse to write, when *Paris* asks his lays!" The rest is a subordinate parenthesis which structurally welds the two couplets together. Another less elaborate example gives a similar total effect:

Yet let not me of grievances complain,
Who (though the meanest of the Muse's train)
Can boast subscriptions to my humble lays,
And mingle profit with my little praise.

(*Epistle to Methuen*, 43-46)

Here the parenthesis does not break over into the second couplet, but it does unify the two by placing "who" in the first couplet as the subject of the verbs in the second. Finally, an instance in which the parenthesis is continued for almost five and a half lines between the main subject and verb:

> Thus the bold traveller, (inur'd to toil,
> Whose steps have printed *Asia's* desert soil,
> The barb'rous *Arabs* haunt; or shiv'ring crost
> Dark *Greenland's* mountains of eternal frost;
> Whom providence in length of years restores
> To the wish'd harbour of his native shores;)
> Sets forth his journals to the publick view,
> To caution, by his woes, the wandring crew.
>
> (*Trivia*, III, 399-406)

But the full interplay of thought, feeling, movement, and music can best be illustrated in a somewhat larger passage:

> Why did *'Change-Alley* waste thy precious Hours,
> Among the Fools who gap'd for golden Show'rs?
> No wonder, if we found some *Poets* there,
> Who live on Fancy, and can feed on Air;
> No wonder, *they* were caught by *South-Sea* Schemes,
> Who ne'er enjoy'd a Guinea, but in Dreams;
> No wonder, *they* their Third Subscriptions sold,
> For Millions of imaginary Gold:
> No wonder that *their* Fancies wild can frame
> Strange Reasons, that a Thing is still the same,
> Though chang'd throughout in Substance and in Name.
> But *you* (whose Judgment scorns Poetick Flights)
> With Contracts furnish Boys for Paper Kites.
>
> (*Epistle to Snow*, 17-29)

An analysis of these lines, which in the 1727 edition comprise a verse paragraph, will not only justify this paragraphing, but will reveal Gay's virtuosity in structural organization. The passage is composed of three sentences: the first couplet, the next nine lines, and the last couplet. The first sentence, a question, logically introduces the second through the key word "Fools"; for the long second sentence is an ironic characterization of one type of fool—the poet. The third sentence presents a contrast (signalized by the conjunction "but"), in which the irony continues and is finally driven home. Within the framework of the first and last couplets the second sentence is balanced and unified by the four-fold repetition of the "No wonder" construction, and the repetition of the word "Fancy" in the fourth and ninth lines strengthens this syntactic coherence. The fourth couplet provides a startling metrical variation: its first line is a normal iambic pentameter, but its second is a sharply contrasting three-stress line, with two accents suppressed. Finally, the entire passage is further distinguished by the varied alliteration of the four consonant sounds *g, f, s,* and *m.* Because of these characteristics, among others, the total effect is rich, subtle, and complex.

II

The great majority of Gay's heroic-couplet poems are narrative, descriptive, or satiric. The narrative poems are mainly translations from Ovid and Ariosto, most of which are inferior compared, for example, to the best of Dryden or of Crabbe. They give the impression of being little better than hack work, even though the Ovid stories (those of "Arachne," "Achelous and Hercules," etc.) were translated by Gay in collaboration with other "most eminent hands." As narratives, they are stiff and static, the couplets heavy and monotonous. I leave out of account as wholly undistinguished the narrative element in *Dione,* Gay's pastoral tragedy in heroic couplets.

There are, however, a few exceptions to this general run of mediocrity in narrative, probably the best of which is "The Story of Cephisa." This version of the Daphne legend recounts, in relatively spirited couplets, Pan's passionate pursuit of the maid, Cephisa, and her subsequent transformation into a plant in order to defeat his purpose. The poem opens with couplets that are appropriately and interestingly varied:

> In western climes where the bright God of day
> Darts on the gladsome earth a warmer ray,
> While smiling Spring led on the jocund hours,
> And early months bestrew'd the fields with flow'rs,
> In bloom of youth *Cephisa*, lovely maid,
> Trac'd the wide lawns, and thro' the forests stray'd.
>
> (1-6)

The thought, rhythm, and music of these lines create a lively tempo, which sets the pace for the subsequent narrative passages. In the first couplet, for example, the meaning of the adjective "bright" in context with the verb "darts" suggests swift movement, and their sounds echo this sense. Rhythmically the substitution of a pyrrhic in the third metrical foot of the first line and a trochee in the first of the second reinforces this lively tempo.

The pace of the narrative itself is best revealed in the following passage, which leads up to the climax of the pursuit:

> With double speed the nymph her course renew'd,
> With double speed the ravisher pursu'd,
> O'er hills and dales they hold the rapid race,
> Till, spent at length, and weary'd with the chace,
> With secret dread she views the sun descend,
> And twilight o'er the earth her veil extend;
> For now the swift pursuer nearer drew,
> And almost touch'd her garments as she flew;
> Wheel'd as she wheel'd, on ev'ry footstep gain'd,
> And no relief nor glimpse of hope remain'd. (77-86)

This is rhetorical and somewhat melodramatic, but it has speed; and the syntax of the sentence, despite the end-stopped couplets, manages a narrative progression, indicated by the signal words "With" (repeated once), "Till," "For now," and the last two "And's." In contrast to the success of this narrative style, consider the following attempt at narrative in a passage from "The Story of Achelous and Hercules":

> Three times in vain he strove my Joints to wrest,
> To force my Hold, and throw me from his Breast;
> The fourth he broke my Gripe, that clasp'd him round,
> Then with new Force he stretch'd me on the Ground;
> Close to my Back the mighty Burthen clung,
> As if a Mountain o'er my Limbs were flung.
> Believe my Tale; nor do I, boastful, aim
> By feign'd Narration to extol my Fame.   (61-68)

Here the language and the couplets are both ill-chosen and inept. The only narrative that merits consideration with "The Story of Cephisa" in terms of heroic-couplet technique is the "True Story of an Apparition," in which at least an impressive atmosphere is created.

Gay's descriptive poems represent a considerably higher level of achievement in the heroic couplet, and among them are some of his better known works. One of these is *Rural Sports*, first published in 1713 and completely revised in 1720. In form *Rural Sports* belongs to the tradition of the descriptive-meditative poem that stems from Denham's *Cooper's Hill*; as such it suggests comparison not only with that poem, but also with *Windsor Forest* by Pope, to whom indeed it is inscribed as a "Georgic."

Like Pope's poem and unlike Denham's, *Rural Sports* is primarily descriptive with incidental philosophizing. The first thirty and the concluding forty-seven lines contain most of the meditation, which may be summed up simply as the repeated assertion of the superiority of country over urban life. This was of course a familiar neo-classic theme, usually illustrated in the anthologies by John Pomfret's poem, *The Choice*. Elsewhere in *Rural Sports* the philosophizing appears occasionally in such passages as the following:

Now night in silent state begins to rise,
And twinkling orbs bestrow th' uncloudy skies;
Her borrow'd lustre growing *Cynthia* lends,
And on the main a glitt'ring path extends;
Millions of worlds hang in the spacious air,
Which round their suns their annual circles steer.
Sweet contemplation elevates my sense,
While I survey the works of providence.
O could the muse in loftier strains rehearse,
The glorious author of the universe,
Who reins the winds, gives the vast ocean bounds,
And circumscribes the floating worlds their rounds,
My soul should overflow in songs of praise,
And my Creator's name inspire my lays!   (107-20)

In terms of the thought, this sonnet-length passage is divided
into an octave of generalized but appropriate description and
a sestet of philosophic meditation. Furthermore, the rhe-
torical exclamatory tone and the ode-like movement of the
couplets give a strong lyrical quality to the meditative second
part.

Also like Pope's, Gay's description in this poem is largely
generalized and denotative. Apart from the natural neo-
classic tendency to use this kind of language, in *Rural Sports*
Gay had a special reason for doing so: the poem is an "imi-
tation" of Pope's own pastorals and of Virgil's *Georgics*.
Early in the poem Gay directly addresses these two masters
in announcing his own purpose:

And the same road ambitiously pursue,
Frequented by the *Mantuan* swain, and you.   (29-30)

This influence of the traditional pastoral appears even more
significantly in a later passage. First Gay describes himself
lying in a meadow reading Virgil, after which he arises and
continues his own description in the Virgilian manner:

Here I peruse the *Mantuan's* Georgic strains,
And learn the labours of *Italian* swains;

In ev'ry page I see new landscapes rise,
And all *Hesperia* opens to my eyes.
I wander o'er the various rural toil,
And know the nature of each different soil:
This waving field is gilded o'er with corn,
That spreading trees with blushing fruit adorn:
Here I survey the purple vintage grow,
Climb round the poles, and rise in graceful row:
Now I behold the steed curvet and bound,
And paw with restless hoof the smoking ground.

(67-78)

In contrast to Gay's purpose in *Rural Sports,* his purpose
in *Trivia* may be called non-imitative realistic description.
The result is a far different and better poem and one of
Gay's best known works. The mock-heroic devices in *Trivia*
are especially noteworthy. There is the invocation to the
muse, the use of the supernatural and the epic simile, the
mythological allusions, and the heightened epic style—all
devoted to a commonplace and trivial subject: walking the
streets of London. However, this poem is not a true mock-
heroic in the sense that *MacFlecknoe, The Dispensary,* and
The Rape of the Lock are: it is rather a descriptive poem with
satiric and mock-heroic elements. The muse in *Trivia* is not
the usual epic muse ironically addressed: she is the Goddess
Trivia herself; and the supernatural interventions (the myth-
ological origin of "pattens," the divine but vulgarized gene-
alogy of the bootblack, etc.) are too crude to be subtly mock-
heroic. But in effect these crudities reëmphasize the essential
realism of the entire poem, throughout which such vivid
details as the following are commonplace:

When fishy stalls with double store are laid;
The golden-belly'd carp, the broad-finn'd maid,
Red-speckled trouts, the salmon's silver joul,
The joynted lobster, and unscaly soale,
And lucious 'scollops, to allure the tastes

Of rigid zealots to delicious fasts;
Wednesdays and *Fridays* you'll observe from hence,
Days, when our sires were doom'd to abstinence.

(II, 413-20)

In addition to the colorful picture, the thought of the third
couplet is, in context, witty and complex. The "rigid zealots"
are the "sires . . . doom'd to abstinence," who are here subtly
ridiculed by means of the paradoxical "delicious fasts."
Though less satiric and more realistic than the traditional
mock-heroic poem, *Trivia* nevertheless ends on a mock-heroic
note, in which the tone of good-humored raillery, character-
istic of Gay, dominates the passage:

And now compleat my gen'rous labours lye,
Finish'd and ripe for immortality.
Death shall entomb in dust this mould'ring frame,
But never reach th' eternal part, my fame.
When Ward and Gibbon, mighty names, are dead;
Or but at *Chelsea* under custards read;
When Criticks crazy bandboxes repair
And Tragedies, turn'd rockets, bounce in air;
High-rais'd on *Fleet-street* posts, consign'd to fame,
This work shall shine, and walkers bless my name.

Gay frequently laughs at others, but, unlike Pope, he never
forgets to laugh also at himself.

It is as a satirist that Gay excels in the heroic couplet,
despite the seemingly formidable competition with Pope and
Dryden. The nature and effects of Gay's satire, due in no
small measure to his handling of the couplet, are distinctive
enough to set him apart from even his strongest competitors
in poetry. In general we may describe Gay's satire as mild
and non-malicious; it gently rebukes rather than stingingly
attacks; and its object is usually the type rather than the
individual. Even Swift's formula—

Yet malice never was his aim;
He lash'd the vice, but spar'd the name—

does not fit Gay, for his satire never lashes, and it is directed not at the vices of man but at the more venial foibles of society. In tone, method, and subject matter this satire belongs in the tradition of Addison, Steele, and Goldsmith rather than that of Pope, Swift, and Churchill. In a very real sense, Gay was the poetic "Mr. Spectator" of his time.

Early in his career Gay wrote *The Fan*, in which, in mock-heroic style, he satirized the use of this fashionable accessory. The tone and attitude are comparable to the treatment of the same subject by Addision. Thus Gay:

> The peeping fan in modern times shall rise,
> Through which unseen the female ogle flies;
> This shall in temples the sly maid conceal,
> And shelter love beneath devotion's veil.
>
> . . . . .
>
> As learned Orators that touch the heart,
> With various action raise their soothing art,
> Both head and hand affect the list'ning throng,
> And humour each expression of the tongue.
> So shall each passion by the fan be seen,
> From noisie anger to the sullen spleen.　　(III, 171-82)

The last couplet summarizes an aspect of the subject which Addison expands in *Spectator* No. 102:

There is an infinite Variety of Motions to be made use of in the *Flutter of a Fan:* There is the angry Flutter, the modest Flutter, the timorous Flutter, the confused Flutter, the merry Flutter, and the amorous Flutter. Not to be tedious, there is scarce any Emotion in the Mind which does not produce a suitable Agitation in the Fan; insomuch that if I only see the Fan of a disciplin'd Lady, I know very well whether she laughs, frowns, or blushes . . .[8]

And a short episode in Gay's *Epistle to Pulteney*, in which he satirizes French audiences who ruin an opera by joining in the singing (lines 185-204), parallels Addison's mild

[8] *The Spectator*, ed. G. Gregory Smith.

ridicule of a lady of quality who, newly returned from France, spoils a scene at the playhouse with her fashionable chatter (*Spectator*, No. 45).[9]

Gay's finest and most characteristic satire appears in his eclogues and epistles—especially in *The Birth of the Squire, The Toilette, The Epistle to William Pulteney,* and *The Epistle to Paul Methuen.* In these we find that mixture of wit, satire, and sympathy which is his most distinctive contribution to heroic-couplet poetry. The peculiar quality of this combination may be sensed in the following lines about the young squire:

> O vent'rous youth, thy thirst of game allay,
> Mayst thou survive the perils of this day!
> He shall survive; and in late years be sent
> To snore away Debates in *Parliament.*   (73-76)

The last line contains the satire, which is mild and witty; but the preceding lines overlay the satire with a concurrent tone of sympathy. In *The Epistle to Pulteney* the following passage reveals the same kind of humorous sympathetic satire:

> Such were our pleasures in the days of yore,
> When am'rous *Charles Britannia's* scepter bore;
> The nightly scene of joy the *Park* was made,
> And Love in couples peopled ev'ry shade.
> But since at Court the rural taste is lost,
> What mighty summs have velvet couches cost!
>
> (127-32)

Here the "Love in couples peopled ev'ry shade," "the rural taste," and the "mighty summs" for "velvet couches" convey in context the peculiar flavor of Gay's criticism of the social scene.

The six poems comprising *The Shepherd's Week* (Sunday was omitted, says Gay dryly, because "ours being sup-

[9] *Op. cit.*

posed to be Christian shepherds, and to be then at worship")
are less successful, although better known, than the satires I
have mentioned. As satire *The Shepherd's Week* is heavy-
handed, farcical, and obvious. For the most part, the humor
is cruder than usual with Gay, and the Spenserian language is
overdone—too much of a good thing. Technically the coup-
lets are undistinguished, perhaps because so much of the
poet's effort went into devising the pastoral trappings. In-
deed, it may be questioned whether the spritely prose
"proeme to the courteous reader" is not more effectively
humorous and satiric than the poems which it introduces.

Many of Gay's poems contain passages of excellent satire
and some of them are entirely satiric, but few of these are
organically well-constructed poems as a whole. The *Epistle
to Paul Methuen* is, however, an exception. It is a relatively
short satire of ninety-eight lines, divided logically into five
parts. The first fourteen lines introduce the subject, a fa-
miliar one in the early eighteenth century:

> When learning droops, and sickens in the land,
> What Patron's found to lend a saving hand?

Part II (lines 15-46) develops this theme by picturing
the slavish conditions under which the modern poet must
write in order to acquire a patron and success. The theme
was, of course, made famous later by Johnson, both in his
letter to Chesterfield and in *The Vanity of Human Wishes:*

> There mark what ills the scholar's life assail,
> Toil, envy, want, the patron, and the jail.

Gay's handling of the subject, though less bitter and epi-
grammatic, is excellent of its kind:

> Yet there are ways for authors to be great;
> Write ranc'rous libels to reform the state:
> Or if you chuse more sure and ready ways,
> Spatter a Minister with fulsome praise:

> Launch out with freedom, flatter him enough;
> Fear not, all men are dedication-proof.
> Be bolder yet, you must go farther still,
> Dip deep in gall thy mercenary quill . . .   (19-26)

The couplets are well managed, with their variations in rhythm, music, and stress; and "Fear not, all men are dedication-proof" comes as close as Gay ever does to epigram in the heroic couplet. After this direct attack, the conclusion of Part II presents a contrast which, however, increases the effectiveness of the satire because it becomes irony, a device used sparingly by Gay in his serious satire:

> Aganst th' ungrateful age these authors roar,
> And fancy learning starves because they're poor.
> Yet why should learning hope success at Court?
> Why should our Patriots vertue's cause support?
> Why to true merit should they have regard?
> They know that vertue is its own reward.   (37-42)

In Part III (lines 47-74) Gay turns from poetry and patrons to the related subject of art and patrons. William Kent in painting and design and "*Palladio's* rules" in architecture are the examples, in the true appreciation of which the patrons Burlington and Chandos are complimented as exceptions to the run of "Patriots." Part IV is brief (lines 75-84) and returns partially to the subject of Part II, for it deals with poets and critics instead of patrons. There is another difference: we have progressed from the general to the specific, so particular poets (Gay's friends) and critics are introduced:

> Had *Pope* with groveling numbers fill'd his page,
> *Dennis* had never kindled into rage.
> 'Tis the sublime that hurts the Critic's ease;
> Write nonsense and he reads and sleeps in peace.
> Were *Prior, Congreve, Swift,* and *Pope* unknown,
> Poor slander-selling *Curll* would be undone.

> He who would free from malice pass his days,
> Must live obscure, and never merit praise.   (75-82)

The concluding Part V is as unusual as it is effective. It is a short animal fable, which allegorically summarizes the point of the whole poem ("But let this tale to valiant vertue tell The daily perils of deserving well"). An untalented and ugly crow speaks to a beautiful singing lark, who answers with the "moral" in the last two couplets:

> My song confines me to the wiry cage,
> My flight provokes the faulcon's fatal rage.
> But as I pass, I hear the fowlers say,
> To shoot at crows is powder flung away.

It is perhaps noteworthy that the first and last parts of this poem contain fourteen lines each and that Root, when considering such sonnet-like units in Pope's work, suggests an analogy with that form.[10] In Gay's two fourteen-line sequences the first divides logically and is paragraphed between an octave and a sestet, and the second divides logically with the conjunction "yet" at the ninth line: "Yet let me pass my life from envy free."

Gay's reputation as a gifted poet of the second order is probably justified by the quality of his work. He was extremely versatile, and is today better known in less competitive areas than that of the heroic couplet—in the operatic lyric and the octosyllabics of *The Fables*. But his achievements in the heroic couplet are greater than has been generally recognized. Technically Gay's management of the heroic couplet is always skillful and, at its best, excellent. In the handful of poems which represent that excellence, he merits inclusion among the masters of the form.

---

[10] "Though Pope was quite regardless of the sonnet form as such, his artistic instinct seems to have led him to flights of song which have a similar extent and a similar unity of movement": *op. cit.*, p. 49.

Chapter III

≈≈≈≈≈≈≈≈≈≈≈≈≈≈≈≈≈≈≈≈≈≈≈≈≈

Johnson: "Pathos in Isolation"

I

ALTHOUGH it is rarely deplored, Samuel Johnson's poetry has been for the most part quietly overlooked or, at best, condescendingly taken for granted. Underlying these views is the tacit critical assumption that in writing poetry Johnson had, in contradistinction to Milton, the use of only his left hand—and a feeble left hand at that! This attitude not only has prevailed from the nineteenth century, but has been reasserted today by Joseph Wood Krutch.[1] It is likely, therefore, to have renewed currency. There is of course no denying that Johnson is greater in prose than in poetry, but it may be questioned whether he was not more ambidextrous than has been generally admitted. In fact, his poetic achievements place him, in this respect, in the august company of Ben Jonson, Dryden, Goldsmith, Coleridge, and Matthew Arnold. And the heroic couplet was his medium *par excellence.*

Of Johnson's poems in this form, the least well known are the four Prologues (for "the Opening of the Theatre in Drury-Lane, 1747," for *Comus*, for *The Good Natur'd Man*, and for *A Word to the Wise*) and the Epilogue "intended to have been spoken by a Lady who was to personate the Ghost of Hermione."[2] Two of these merit consideration among

[1] In *Samuel Johnson*, pp. 60-66.

[2] A fifth Prologue has recently been discovered and attributed to Johnson by Mary E. Knapp. It was found in the Folger Shakespeare Library, endorsed in

Johnson's best work, and all of them in parts reveal characteristics of his genius.

In the Epilogue the dominant note is flattery, at which Johnson could hardly be expected to excel. Awkward compliment, excessive rhetoric, and heavy-handed humor take up most of the poem, as the following passage indicates:

> For kind, for tender nymphs the myrtle blooms,
> And weaves her bending boughs in pleasing glooms;
> Perennial roses deck each purple vale,
> And scents ambrosial breathe in every gale:
> Far hence are banish'd vapours, spleen, and tears,
> Tea, scandal, ivory teeth, and languid airs;
> No pug, nor favourite Cupid there enjoys
> The balmy kiss, for which poor Thyrsis dies;
> Form'd to delight, they use no foreign arms,
> Nor torturing whalebones pinch them into charms.[3]

And the famous clumsy logic with which *The Vanity of Human Wishes* opens is repeated in miniature in this poem: "Vexation, Fury, Jealousy, Despair, Vex ev'ry eye, and ev'ry bosom tear." Yet in the midst of this mediocrity, the following couplets stand out for their technical strength and Johnsonian excellence:

> But cruel virgins meet severer fates;
> Expell'd and exil'd from the blissful seats,
> To dismal realms, and regions void of peace,
> Where furies ever howl, and serpents hiss.
> O'er the sad plains perpetual tempests sigh;
> And pois'nous vapours, black'ning all the sky,
> With livid hue the fairest face o'ercast,
> And every beauty withers at the blast . . .   (28-35)

Garrick's hand: "Prologue by Mr. Sam: Johnson for *Lethe*," a satiric farce performed in 1740 at the Drury Lane. The poem of eight couplets is in no way exceptional, although its style and thought could readily make it Johnson's. It is printed in *TLS*, XLVI, 9.

[3] Lines 14-23: unless otherwise indicated, all references to Johnson's work are from *The Poems of Samuel Johnson*, ed. David Nichol Smith and Edward L. McAdam.

It is noteworthy that Johnson is more successful and at ease in these "dismal realms" than he is in the "blissful seats" of happiness, where a lighter touch and a less tragic view of life than his are prerequisite.

Johnson's Prologue, written for the opening of the Drury Lane, is a brief "progress of poesy" on the stage. It proceeds from Shakespeare and Jonson, through the Restoration into the eighteenth century, predicts the future of the drama, and ends with a Johnsonian exhortation to the audience: "Bid scenic Virtue form the rising Age, And Truth diffuse her Radiance from the Stage." This chronological development in seven verse-paragraphs gives the poem an obvious mechanical structure.

The couplets are for the most part traditional and undistinguished. There are, however, occasional flashes of Johnson's tone and manner, as in the lines on Shakespeare:

> Each Change of many-colour'd Life he drew,
> Exhausted Worlds, and then imagin'd new:
> Existence saw him spurn her bounded Reign,
> And panting Time toil'd after him in vain . . .   (3-6)

The use of personified abstractions to achieve effects that are vast yet vivid and the slowing down of the tempo to the organ-like music of the last line are characteristic of Johnson's style at its best. Also characteristic is his manner of registering disapproval of Restoration drama; he describes its downfall through personification and a kind of indirection of thought:

> Till Shame regain'd the Post that Sense betray'd,
> And Virtue call'd Oblivion to her Aid.   (27-28)

These are, however, but flashes—for the most part the Prologue is mediocre.

Little more can be said for the short Prologue to Goldsmith's comedy, *The Good Natur'd Man*. Structurally this poem is unified by the expanded parallel between two of the "busy candidates for power and fame": the politician and the dramatist. Both ultimately depend for success upon the ordinary man as voter and audience. There is, however, one difference between the office seeker and the playwright: "The bard may supplicate, but cannot bribe." In the end, therefore, he "Trusts without fear, to merit, and to you." The Prologue opens on the note of Johnsonian pessimism and solemnity:

> Prest by the load of life, the weary mind
> Surveys the general toil of human kind;

after which the traditional couplets march to their conclusion with dignity if without distinction.

The two remaining Prologues are more successful as heroic-couplet poems. The Prologue to *A Word to the Wise* is well constructed, having a twenty-line development of one theme and a generalized conclusion. The theme is the relationship between the dramatist, now dead, and his audience. Underlying this subject is the fact that when Hugh Kelly was alive his play had been "hooted from the stage." First the author-audience relationship is itself dramatized figuratively as a battle between them; so to the audience Johnson says:

> A generous foe regards, with pitying eye,
> The man whom fate has laid, where all must lye. (5-6)

The ingredients of this situation, presenting a contrast between life and death and allowing for appropriate reflections upon fame and the vanity of human wishes, were made to order for a mind like Johnson's His development of the theme takes the form of an appeal to the audience in terms of the dead author:

> Where aught of bright, or fair, the piece displays,
> Approve it only—'tis too late to praise.
> If want of skill, or want of care appear,

> Forbear to hiss—the Poet cannot hear.
> By all, like him, must praise and blame be found;
> At best, a fleeting gleam, or empty sound.   (15-20)

The dominant effect of these lines in context is a peculiar and powerful kind of pathos—peculiar in that it is characteristic of Johnson, powerful in that it verges on the tragic.

Technically the couplets of this Prologue reveal Johnson's mature style. Metrical variety appears in the frequent shifts between five- and four-stress lines, the latter with one normal accent suppressed. Two of the lines contain extra syllables; there are occasional trochaic substitutions; and although the caesura varies from the end of the first foot to the end of the fourth, it occurs most often near the middle of the line. All couplets are of course rigidly end-stopped. Balance and contrast are noteworthy in the last quotation above, in which the first couplet as a whole and in parts syntactically parallels the second, but the ideas are in direct contrast.

More subtle effects of music and movement appear in the following passage:

> To Wit, reviving from its author's dust,
> Be kind, ye judges, or at least be just:
> Let no resentful petulance invade
> Th' oblivious grave's inviolable shade.   (7-10)

The speed of the first couplet is in sharp contrast to the slowness of the second, partly because of the predominance of short vowels in the one and long vowels in the other. But the total effect is more complex than this, involving the interplay of the music and meaning with the movement. In this interplay, the *s* and *v* sounds are particularly important, as is the arrangement of the monosyllabic in contrast to the polysyllabic words. Within the passage the thought moves from one extreme expressed by the various meanings of "wit" to the other conveyed by all the implications of the "oblivious" grave. And the last line, with its slow literally used latinate polysyllables, is pure Johnson.

In the great Prologue to *Comus* appear most of the qualities that inform Johnson's best poetry. It was written for a benefit performance of *Comus* in honor of Milton's granddaughter, an occasion which well may have prompted Johnson to extend himself. Structurally this Prologue of thirty-eight lines may be divided into three parts: the general appeal to the audience (lines 1-14), the praise of Milton (15-22), and the concluding appeal on behalf of the granddaughter (23-38). The final couplet reasserts the debt of the living to the dead, and returns us to the beginning by re-addressing the audience:

> Yours is the Charge, ye Fair, ye Wise, ye Brave!
> 'Tis yours to crown Desert—beyond the Grave!

The opening appeal attains a level of high seriousness— a tone that the couplet form makes "heroic" in the best sense. Addressing the audience as patriot Englishmen "whose Bosoms beat at Milton's Name," Johnson says:

> Immortal Patrons of succeeding Days,
> Attend this Prelude of perpetual Praise!
> Let Wit, condemn'd the feeble War to wage
> With close Malevolence, or public Rage;
> Let Study, worn with Virtue's fruitless Lore,
> Behold this Theatre, and grieve no more.
> This Night, distinguish'd by your Smile, shall tell,
> That never Briton can in vain excel;
> The slighted Arts Futurity shall trust,
> And rising Ages hasten to be just.   (5-14)

The rhetorical formality of these lines is noteworthy. It arises mainly from the balanced syntax of the second and third couplets, in which the personification is also concentrated; from the latinate polysyllabic vocabulary; and from the organ music (the slow and solemn movement) of the

entire passage. In terms of the thought, the stoical John-
sonian pessimism (Wit waging feeble war "With close
Malevolence, or public Rage," Study "worn with Virtue's
fruitless Lore") is sharply contrasted with the tribute to
Comus ("this Prelude of perpetual Praise") and with the
concluding ideas ("That never Briton can in vain excel . . .
And rising Ages hasten to be just"). The presence of this
contrast adds a dramatic note to the entire passage.

In the second part of the Prologue, devoted to the meas-
ured praise of Milton, the grand style is continued:

> At length our mighty Bard's victorious Lays
> Fill the loud Voice of universal Praise,
> And baffled Spite, with hopeless Anguish dumb,
> Yields to Renown the Centuries to come.
> With ardent Haste, each Candidate of Fame
> Ambitious catches at his tow'ring Name:
> He sees, and pitying sees, vain Wealth bestow
> Those pageant Honours which he scorn'd below.
>
> (15-22)

There is less emphasis, in this passage, on formal rhetoric—
less use of personification and syntactic balance. But the
couplets, end-stopped and majestic, march to their conclusion,
ringing not like a bell (as do Dryden's at his best), but with
their own special kind of magniloquence. The one couplet
using personification is especially effective. Finally, in the
last couplet reappear the Johnsonian awareness of the life-
death contrast and its accompanying pathos, verging on
tragedy.

The third part of the Prologue is related to the second
through the assertion of a contrast: Milton's great fame ver-
sus his granddaughter's obscurity (lines 23-26), after which
her virtues are described, and the final appeal is made on her
behalf. In keeping with the vastness and nobility of the en-
tire Prologue, she is last pictured as receiving the tribute of
nations:

> Secure with Peace, with Competence to dwell,
> While tutelary Nations guard her Cell.

The couplets of this Prologue reveal most of the characteristics of the earlier masters of the form. There are almost equal numbers of five- and four-stress lines, a half dozen instances of trochaic substitution, several lines with extra syllables, and striking uses of alliteration and special syntactic constructions. Johnson was not an innovator in form, as was, for example, his contemporary Charles Churchill. But as all of these Prologues reveal, in whole or in part, Johnson turns the technically traditional couplet into something rich and strange through the power of his mind and personality. In his hands it achieves a solemn stateliness, a slow-paced resonance, a universality in meaning, and a tone of "pathos in isolation"[4] that, at its best, is unique. In the two longer poems that are usually considered his major work, these qualities and their ramifications stand out even more clearly, and give final proof for the contention that he is a master of the heroic-couplet poem.

II

No one who attends to the music of *London* and *The Vanity of Human Wishes*, particularly as it influences the total meaning, can take seriously the charge that Johnson had a bad ear. Not only in numerous passages where the sound harmoniously echoes the sense, but also in his revisions can we observe his artistry. In the first edition of *The Vanity of Human Wishes*, line 150 appears as,

> And Sloth's bland Opiates shed their Fumes in vain.

Later this line becomes:

> And Sloth effuse her opiate fumes in vain.

In the revision there are fewer *s* sounds, the alliterative "effuse-fumes" is added, the number of monosyllables is re-

---

[4] The phrase is Winters': *op. cit.*, p. 137.

duced from eight to six, and the more harmonious latinate verb "effuse" replaces the Anglo-Saxon "shed." In total effect these changes greatly improve the music and emotional tone, making them more directly reinforce the thought of the line. Consider, for example, the differences in context between "effuse" and "shed."[5]

The most important single effect that Johnson achieves— the effect of "pathos in isolation"—stems directly from his mastery of tone and music. Into the didactic-satiric poem he introduces lyrical elements of deep and powerful significance. The following passage from *London* is a minor instance:

> Illustrious Edward! from the realms of day,
> The land of heroes and of saints survey;
> Nor hope the British lineaments to trace,
> The rustick grandeur, or the surly grace,
> But lost in thoughtless ease, and empty show,
> Behold the warrior dwindled to a beau;
> Sense, freedom, piety, refin'd away,
> Of France the mimick, and of Spain the prey. (99-106)

The lyrical tone of these lines is strongly supported by their movement, which itself has a special characteristic. It is the suppression of the third or fourth normal stress in six out of the eight lines (lines 1, 2, 3, 4, 6, and 8). Consequently in the second half of each of these lines there occurs a pyrrhic foot of two unstressed syllables, the effect of which is a pronounced anapestic rhythm. In the greater passages from

---

[5] Consider also the awkwardness of sound and monotonous repetition of rhymes in the following first-edition version of lines 355-58:

> Implore his aid, in his decisions rest,
> Secure whate'er he gives, he gives the best.
> Yet with the sense of sacred presence prest,
> When strong devotion fills thy glowing breast,
> Pour forth thy fervours, etc.

And see Smith, *op. cit.*, pp. 31-55.

The Vanity of Human Wishes this lyrical movement is everywhere present[6]—in, for example, the couplets:

> Must helpless man, in ignorance sedate,
> Roll darkling down the torrent of his fate?
> Must no dislike alarm, no wishes rise,
> No cries attempt the mercies of the skies? (345-48)

And particularly in the magnificent conclusion of the poem, in which half of the last twelve lines contain this pyrrhic third or fourth foot.

The impersonal and didactic kind of poetry that Johnson wrote is closest in style and language to that of Pope in the moral essays. Particularly must the generalized vocabulary that both used be understood and accepted if we are to defend Johnson as poet. Neo-classic critical theory approved a relatively high degree of abstractness in the poetic vocabulary. The Romantic revolt was in part a protest against these abstractions, which was one reason for the attack on poetic diction. The kind of imagery used in the eighteenth century tended to support this high degree of abstraction by stressing the similarities between the "tenor" and "vehicle" of the comparison; for the more obviously alike things are, the higher the degree of abstract language in which they can be expressed. The opposite tendency ("the discovery of occult resemblances in things apparently unlike") Johnson specifically repudiates in his criticism of the metaphysical poets.

There is no basic reason why either highly abstract or relatively concrete language should not be appropriate in poetry. Indeed, I. A. Richards asserts categorically that "the

---

[6] Krutch sees nothing lyrical in these poems, because they were not written by "the lyric poet who infuses everything with a personal emotion" (*op. cit.*, p. 62). In "Tradition and the Individual Talent" T. S. Eliot flatly contradicts this view: "The emotion of art is impersonal." Krutch is either judging by Romantic standards or he is denying the existence of lyricism outside of lyric poetry as such. In either case, his qualifications for dealing with neo-classic poetry as critic, not historian, would seem open to question.

language of the greatest poetry is frequently abstract in the extreme."[7] It is therefore an unreasonably narrow critical view that would *ipso facto* relegate didactic poetry to a position of inferiority on the grounds of its abstract vocabulary. If, on the other hand, the objection is based on excessive moralizing (the "moral tag"), the criticism is not directed against the poetry because it is didactic, but because it is simply bad poetry.

Additional light on the nature of poetic language appears in a familiar contrast between Swinburne and Dryden:

Swinburne was also a master of words, but Swinburne's words are all suggestion and no denotation; if they suggest nothing, it is because they suggest too much. Dryden's words, on the other hand, are precise, they state immensely, but their suggestiveness is almost nothing.[8]

The way in which didactic poetry states immensely but suggests little, may be further clarified by a comparison of Donne and Johnson. In the last stanza of Donne's "Hymn to God the Father," the subject is man's fear of the unknown future:

> I have a sinne of feare, that when I have spunne
>   My last thred, I shall perish on the shore;
> But sweare by Thyselfe, that at my death Thy sonne
>   Shall shine as he shines now, and heretofore;
>   And, having done that, Thou hast done,
>   I feare no more.

This subject is one which the didactic poet might choose to interpret, but he would never proceed in this manner; for here the language states and suggests on different levels of meaning simultaneously. The images, for example, function on physical and metaphysical planes, culminating in the powerful intentional ambiguity of "Thou hast done."

---

[7] *The Philosophy of Rhetoric*, p. 129.
[8] Eliot, *Homage to John Dryden*, p. 22.

The concluding lines from *The Vanity of Human Wishes*
interpret a similar subject ("Where then shall Hope and
Fear their objects find?") in a very different manner:

> Yet when the sense of sacred presence fires,
> And strong devotion to the skies aspires,
> Pour forth thy fervours for a healthful mind,
> Obedient passions, and a will resign'd;
> For love, which scarce collective man can fill;
> For patience sov'reign o'er transmuted ill;
> For faith, that panting for a happier seat,
> Counts death kind Nature's signal of retreat:
> These goods for man the laws of heav'n ordain,
> These goods he grants, who grants the pow'r to gain;
> With these celestial wisdom calms the mind,
> And makes the happiness she does not find.   (357-68)

Here all the significant words are abstractions whose mean-
ings remain on one level. They "state immensely, but their
suggestiveness is almost nothing"—such words as "strong de-
votion," "obedient passions," "love," "collective man," "pa-
tience," "faith," "death," "the laws of heav'n," "celestial
wisdom," "happiness," etc. There is in this passage little
heterogeneity of ideas and no use of intentional ambiguity.
Instead of making the denotative meanings motivate appro-
priate emotions on other levels, Johnson selects words that
denote emotion as well as thought. This concentration and
directness create a powerful and appropriate interpretation of
the experience: the result is didactic poetry of a high order.

Johnson's didacticism does not therefore leave his poetry
coldly intellectual. In his hands, the generalized vocabulary
becomes an instrument for the triple communication of
thought, feeling, and music:

> Must helpless man, in ignorance sedate,
> Roll darkling down the torrent of his fate?

The emotion communicated by abstract words arises from conceptual meanings: as we have said, the thought itself denotes the emotion. In the above couplet, "helpless man" is an abstract phrase that conveys the feelings of pity for such men and fear for ourselves in such a predicament. These are general feelings communicated by the isolated phrase. In context, however, these feelings are limited, sharpened, and deepened by the surrounding ideas and their accompanying emotions. The phrase "in ignorance sedate" qualifies the feeling of pity for the man by giving the reason (ignorance) for his helplessness and by qualifying that reason with the word "sedate," meaning "calm" or "unperturbed." The second line further qualifies our feelings for him by making his situation heroic.

In this couplet Johnson combines directness and indirectness of expression by using the direct conceptual modifiers "helpless" and "in ignorance sedate" and the indirect perceptual image, "Roll darkling down the torrent of his fate." But the indirectness of the image verges on direct denotative communication because of its obvious and commonplace character.[9] The preponderance of similarity between the focal points of the image makes it so homogeneous that communication is practically on one level, in contrast, for example, to the heterogeneity of metaphysical imagery.

Structurally *London* and *The Vanity of Human Wishes*, like the best poems of Dryden and Pope, make use of the principle of contrast to create tensions that become powerfully dramatic. Not all contrasts produce tensions—only those which set up dynamic interplays of thought, feeling, and music. The familiar Swedish Charles passage in *The Vanity of Human Wishes* is a case in point. Charles XII is presented as a warrior hero with "A frame of adamant, a soul of fire." In the first half of the passage he gains glorious victories; in the second half he goes down in humiliating de-

[9] Miss Rosemond Tuve's convincing argument for the conceptual use of imagery further strengthens the case for didactic poetry: see *Elizabethan and Metaphysical Imagery*, pp. 251-410.

feat. What is emphasized is the one-sidedness of Charles, which precipitates his downfall. In terms of the whole poem, this one-sidedness emerges from Charles' pursuit of military glory at the expense of true worth, which is to be found only in obscurity: "Slow rises worth, by poverty depress'd." The operations of "the warrior's pride" are thus set over against those of the virtuous man, as pictured in *London*:

> Couldst thou resign the park and play content
> For the fair banks of Severn or of Trent.
>
> . . . .
>
> There ev'ry bush with nature's musick rings,
> There ev'ry breeze bears health upon its wings;
> On all thy hours security shall smile,
> And bless thine evening walk and morning toil.
>
> (210-23)

In the sharp contrast between the victorious and the vanquished Charles, the two sides are not left statically opposed; for there follows a series of questions (beginning "But did not Chance at length her error mend?") which momentarily recall the successful hero of the first part, only to drop him into the tragedy of defeat.

Similarly in the portrait of Wolsey the most obvious tensions arise from the contrast between the heights and depths of his career. Wolsey in defeat is preoccupied with his former state and the cause for his downfall: "remember'd folly stings, And his last sighs reproach the faith of kings." Thus in the mind of Wolsey the opposites dramatically coexist. More subtle tensions develop from the play of the satire on the various aspects of Wolsey's career. At the beginning he is pictured "in full-blown dignity," a phrase that combines compliment with a hint of satire. Later "Still to new heights his restless wishes tow'r": "restless wishes" clearly foreshadows "the pride of awful state" which goeth before a fall. Finally, the criticism of Wolsey's principles and character becomes outright in the following couplet:

> For why did Wolsey, near the steeps of fate,
> On weak foundations raise th' enormous weight?
>
> (125-26)

And we know that Wolsey's tragedy was one of character as well as fate.

Even within couplets these tensions point up the form and sharpen the satire. Note the following from *London:*

> Here malice, rapine, accident conspire,
> And now a rabble rages, now a fire;
> Their ambush here relentless ruffians lay,
> And here the fell attorney prowls for prey,
> Here falling houses thunder on your head,
> And here a female atheist talks you dead.   (13-18)

In the second line the thought contrast is between the animate and inanimate phenomena of a rabble and a fire raging. This contrast, in the presence of the more obvious similarities, provides a mild dramatic shock. Likewise but more sharply the lines of the third couplet create tension through the contrasts in meaning, while the alliteration of "falling houses" and "female atheist" binds them together. Note also the tension through balance and antithesis in the following couplet:

> Exalt each trifle, ev'ry vice adore,
> Your taste in snuff, your judgment in a whore. (148-49)

Finally, more subtle interplays of meaning occur in, for example, the unexpectedness of "menial" in the following lines from *The Vanity of Human Wishes:*

> The regal palace, the luxurious board,
> The liv'ried army, and the menial lord.   (115-16)

Another noteworthy structural device in the poems is that of syntactic parallelism. Often the thought unity of verse paragraphs will be further strengthened by the repetition of

one or more syntactic constructions, as in the following from
London:

> Has heaven reserv'd, in pity to the poor,
> *No* pathless waste, or undiscover'd shore;
> *No* secret island in the boundless main?
> *No* peaceful desart yet unclaim'd by Spain?
> Quick let us rise, the happy seats explore,
> And bear oppression's insolence no more.
> This mournful truth is ev'ry where confess'd,
> Slow rises worth, by poverty depress'd:
> But here more slow, *where* all are slaves to gold,
> *Where* looks are merchandise, and smiles are sold;
> *Where* won by bribes, by flatteries implor'd,
> The groom retails the favours of his lord.   (170-81)

I have italicized the key words to the syntax, in addition to
which the three-fold repetition of the rhetorical question re-
inforces this kind of structural unity. In *The Vanity of
Human Wishes* occur the two couplets:

> Yet should thy soul indulge the gen'rous heat,
> Till captive Science yields her last retreat;
>
> .   .   .   .   .
>
> Yet hope not life from grief or danger free,
> Nor think the doom of man revers'd for thee; (143-56)

between which is a five-fold repetition of the subjunctive
"should" construction. And finally, in the following lines
from *London*, note the interweaving of the "some" and
"where" constructions:

> Grant me, kind heaven, to find *some* happier place,
> *Where* honesty and sense are no disgrace;
> *Some* pleasing bank where verdant osiers play,
> *Some* peaceful vale with nature's paintings gay;
> *Where* once the harrass'd Briton found repose,
> And safe in poverty defy'd his foes;
> *Some* secret cell, ye pow'rs, indulgent give . . .   (43-49)

In addition to this parallelism, syntactic balance and antithesis are also hallmarks of Johnson's style, as, for example, in the following passage from *The Vanity of Human Wishes:*

> But grant, the virtues of a temp'rate prime
> Bless with an age exempt from scorn or crime;
> An age that melts with unperceiv'd decay,
> And glides in modest Innocence away:
> Whose peaceful day Benevolence endears,
> Whose night congratulating Conscience cheers;
> The gen'ral fav'rite as the gen'ral friend:
> Such age there is, and who shall wish its end?
> Yet ev'n on this her load Misfortune flings,
> To press the weary minutes flagging wings:
> New sorrow rises as the day returns,
> A sister sickens, or a daughter mourns.
> Now kindred Merit fills the sable bier,
> Now lacerated Friendship claims a tear.
> Year chases year, decay pursues decay,
> Still drops some joy from with'ring life away. (291-306)

Here the thought and mood are reversed at the middle of the passage with the conjunction "yet," and certain key words are repeated with contrasting meanings. In the third line "decay" is pleasant because "unperceiv'd"; in the fifteenth "decay pursues decay" in a highly perceived and painful manner. In the fifth line we are given a "peaceful day Benevolence endears," but in the eleventh "New sorrow rises as the day returns." And within this syntax of the passage-as-a-whole the couplets, singly and in groups, have their own carefully ordered balance, antithesis, and parallelism.

Not only in sections of various kinds, but also as wholes many of Johnson's poems are well constructed. We have seen that most of his Prologues possess a clear-cut structural unity. A similar analysis will reveal similar unity in *The Vanity of Human Wishes.* In terms of thought development, this poem of 368 lines may be divided into eight parts as follows. Introductory Part I (the first forty-eight lines) presents the general theme illustrated by a series of brief "observations." The general theme is, of course, that "hope and fear, desire and hate, O'erspread with snares the clouded maze of fate." The conclusion of this section sets the stage for Part III, which deals with Cardinal Wolsey as statesman:

> Yet still one gen'ral cry the skies assails,
> And gain and grandeur load the tainted gales;
> Few know the toiling statesman's fear or care,
> Th' insidious rival and the gaping heir.   (45-48)

Part II (49-72) interrupts the development from Parts I to III by introducing the first of the two philosophic attitudes that dominate the poem. Through the eyes of the laughing cynic Democritus, we are invited to,

> See motley life in modern trappings dress'd,
> And feed with varied fools th' eternal jest.

Part III (73-134) moves from the broad opening theme to a consideration of one aspect of it: the hopes and fears of the statesman, symbolized in the career of Wolsey. Part IV (135-74) deals with another aspect of the general theme: the sad and unmerited fate of the Scholar, "Toil, envy, want, the patron, and the jail."

In Part V (175-254) the fate of warriors is introduced as another major example of the main theme. Most famous among them is of course "Swedish Charles," but also mentioned are Xerxes and Charles Albert of Bavaria. Part VI (255-90) pictures the Man of Wealth in his last years, when "Unnumber'd maladies his joints invade," leaving him only his avarice to die with. Part VII (291-342), after a brief respite from this sad variety of woe, concentrates on the ephemeral nature of Beauty, which at last "falls, betray'd, despis'd, distress'd, And hissing Infamy proclaims the rest."

The last part, in answering the question raised by all the foregoing vanities of human wishes—the question:

Must helpless man, in ignorance sedate,
Roll darkling down the torrent of his fate?—

emphasizes the second of the two philosophic attitudes that dominate the poem: Johnson's own form of Christian stoicism, which rises to a noble climax in the last twelve lines. In structure, therefore, the first two parts and the last one become a framework within which the five central parts operate. These five illustrate the general theme in the following areas: the Statesman, the Scholar, the Warrior, the Man of Wealth, and the great Beauty. Other minor illustrations and variations on these themes embroider the main closely related ideas; but the whole, although rich and complex, remains unified.

If, as Krutch insists, "neoclassical poetry had entered into a decadent stage" by the time *London* appeared in 1738, then of course he is committed to a very qualified approval of *The Vanity of Human Wishes*. "One superiority over *London* it certainly has," he says: "it is no mere rhetorical exercise . . . the one poem is fundamentally sincere, the other fundamentally artificial."[10] Even apart from the specific merits of Johnson's two poems, this view of neo-classic poetry before mid-century must ignore the virtues of Churchill's and Goldsmith's work, to say nothing of those of Crabbe sixty years later. In the light of the present study, such a view is woefully wide of the mark; and the virtues of Johnson's finest poem reinforce this critical assumption.

In *The Vanity of Human Wishes* all the characteristics of Johnson's mastery of the heroic couplet are present. The broad philosophic subject is interpreted in the overlapping territory of the didactic-lyric; the generalized vocabulary states immensely with a minimum of suggestion; the sound and movement are Johnson's own special kind of organ music. Technically the couplets exploit one aspect of the

---

[10] *Op. cit.*, pp. 64-65.

tradition stemming from Pope, the aspect represented in the best passages of the *Essay on Man* and particularly in the conclusion of *The Dunciad*. In Johnson's poem the couplets become masterfully "heroic," and are made to state the most profound truths about human limitations in terms of the tragic awareness of those limitations by one man. The personal (that which is lyric) and the philosophic (that which is universal) are fused into the impersonality of great art. The result is surely one of the great poems of the language.

❦❧❦❧❦❧❦❧❦❧❦❧❦❧❦❧❦❧❦❧❦❧❦❧❦❧❦❧❦❧❦❧❦❧

Chapter IV

Churchill: The Triumph of Irony

I

OF ALL the later masters of the heroic couplet, Charles Churchill has been by far the most neglected. In his own day the most feared of satirists and the most famous of poets, he died in 1764 at the height of his career, and a half century later his reputation had so declined that Byron, visiting his grave at Dover, sensed the tragedy of his fate: "The Glory and the Nothing of a Name." Yet in the quality and quantity of his work, few contemporaries equaled him as a poet and none surpassed him as a satirist.

In terms of the neo-classic tradition, the work of Churchill differs from that of Gay and Johnson because it stems from both Dryden and Pope. Furthermore, Churchill's poetry is the kind that seems disarmingly simple and easily placed, and Churchill himself was one of those poets who seem to reveal themselves by frequent self-criticism in their work. But taking his self-criticism at its face value has strengthened two misconceptions about his poetry: that it is more indebted to Dryden than to Pope, and that it is cruder and more inferior than it actually is.

Churchill's most explicit statement of his preference for Dryden appears in *The Apology:*

> Here let me bend, great Dryden, at thy shrine,
> Thou dearest name to all the tuneful nine.
> What if some dull lines in cold order creep,

And with his theme the poet seems to sleep?
Still, when his subject rises proud to view,
With equal strength the poet rises too:
With strong invention, noblest vigour fraught,
Thought still springs up and rises out of thought;
Numbers ennobling numbers in their course,
In varied sweetness flow, in varied force;
The powers of genius and of judgment join,
And the whole Art of Poetry is thine.[1]

In this passage Churchill places Dryden far above Pope,
whom indeed he damns with faint praise.[2] Technically,
however, his tribute to Dryden is distinctly in the manner
of Pope. In nine of the twelve lines the caesura falls near
the center, after the fourth or fifth syllable, a regularity more
common to Pope than to Dryden. In both line and couplet
the thought and syntax are carefully balanced. Note, for
instance, the balance of phrases in the two halves of most of
the lines: "dearest name"–"tuneful nine," "dull lines"– "cold
order," "strong invention"–"noblest vigour," "varied sweet-
ness"–"varied force," "of genius"–"of judgment." Note also
the repetition of words within the line to give the effect of
an echo: "thought" in the eighth, "numbers" in the ninth,
and "varied" in the tenth lines. In the entire tribute to
Dryden, alliteration is strongly marked and all the couplets
are rigidly end-stopped.

Furthermore, the thought of the passage owes more to
Pope than to any other single source. "Dull lines in cold
order creep, And with his theme the poet seems to sleep"
comes mainly from "ten low words oft creep in one dull
line" and:

[1] Lines 376-87: for all references to Churchill's work I use the *Poems of
Charles Churchill*, ed. James Laver.

[2] In the lines preceding those on Dryden:

> In polish'd numbers and majestic sound,
> Where shall thy rival, Pope! be ever found?
> But whilst each line with equal beauty flows,
> E'en excellence, unvaried, tedious grows . . .

> But in such lays as neither ebb, nor flow,
> Correctly cold and regularly low,
> That shunning faults, one quiet tenor keep;
> We cannot blame indeed—but we may sleep.
>
> (*An Essay on Criticism*, 347 and 239-42)

The "creep–sleep" and "fraught–thought" rhymes occur together (with different contexts, however) in the same passage from Pope.[3]   And the last three of Churchill's couplets are indebted to the famous lines:

> And praise the easy vigour of a line,
> Where Denham's strength, and Waller's sweetness join.
>
> (*An Essay on Criticism*, 360-61)

> Britain to soft refinements less a foe,
> Wit grew polite, and numbers learn'd to flow.
> Waller was smooth; but Dryden taught to join
> The varying verse, the full-resounding line,
> The long majestic march, and energy divine.
>
> (*To Augustus*, 265-69)

Here the ideas of numbers flowing, Waller's "sweetness" and Denham's "strength" (equivalent to Churchill's "sweetness" and "force"), and the "varying verse" reappear, with their own variations, of course, in Churchill.   Indeed it might almost be said that Churchill uses this praise of Dryden in the manner of Pope to convict the latter of his own inferiority!

Churchill's praise of Dryden does, however, identify one of his great models.   Occasionally in the work of Churchill, as in that of Dryden, the couplet is almost wholly subordinated to the larger verse paragraph by means of enjambment and the unrestricted caesura.[4]   In the following passage Churchill describes conditions under Charles I:

---

[3] *An Essay on Criticism*, 347, 239-42, and 354-55.

[4] "Dryden was a believer in significant variety of accent.   Pope . . . recognized three places within the heroic couplet where pauses might come . . . Dryden knew no limits of the kind.   The freedom of blank verse seems to have been in his thoughts.   His pauses come anywhere": Van Doren, *op. cit.*, p. 80.

> Those who, the general good their real aim,
> Sought in their country's good their monarch's fame;
> Those who were anxious for his safety; those
> Who were induced by duty to oppose,
> Their truth suspected, and their worth unknown,
> He held as foes and traitors to his throne,
> Nor found his fatal error till the hour
> Of saving him was gone and past; till power
> Had shifted hands, to blast his hapless reign,
> Making their faith and his repentence vain.
>
> (*Gotham*, II, 501-10)

The run-on couplets weld these lines into a single unit, and the caesura shifts back and forth from the second syllable, at one extreme, to the ninth at the other. Compared to Dryden and Pope, Churchill uses a higher percentage of enjambed couplets; but he is not so different from Dryden in this respect as has been assumed.[5] One indication that enjambment in Churchill is the exception is the fact that full stops within lines are in his work comparatively rare.

To secure change of pace within the couplet, Churchill employs latinate polysyllabic words. Pope of course uses this device, but with Dryden, who first developed it out of Virgil, it is more characteristic; in *Absalom and Achitophel*, for example:

> To head the faction while their zeal was hot,
> And popularly prosecute the plot.

The practice in Churchill is similar:

> Hibernia, famed, 'bove every other grace,
> For matchless intrepidity of face.
>
> (*Rosciad*, 339-40)

> Who often, but without success, have pray'd
> For apt Alliteration's artful aid.
>
> (*Prophecy*, 85-86)

---

[5] Churchill's use of the enjambed couplet varies from about 5 per cent in *The Rosciad* to about 28 per cent in *The Farewell*; in *Absalom and Achitophel*, Part I, the percentage is about eleven. For an analysis and interpretation of Churchill's use of enjambment, see Earl R. Wasserman, "The Return of the Enjambed Couplet," *E L H*, VII, 239-52.

That grave inflexibility of soul,
Which Reason can't convince, nor fear control.

(*Gotham*, III, 335-36)

Know (which few kings, alas! have ever known)
How affability becomes a throne.

(*Gotham*, III, 641-42)

The effect of the polysyllables adds speed and flexibility, making one member of the couplet contrast sharply with the other.

Churchill's style is highly rhetorical, a characteristic that links him not only with Dryden, but with his other well-known prepossession: the drama. *The Rosciad*, a satire on contemporary actors, made Churchill famous overnight; and his interest in the theatre continued throughout his brief career. It would not be surprising, therefore, to find this interest reflected in his manner of writing. Apart from subject matter, both drama and melodrama appear in the rhetorical and often bombastic qualities of his verse:

Let Heaven in vengeance arm all Nature's host,
Those servants who their Maker know, who boast
Obedience as their glory, and fulfill
Unquestion'd, their great Master's sacred will;
Let raging winds root up the boiling deep,
And, with destruction big, o'er Gotham sweep;
Let rains rush down, till Faith, with doubtful eye,
Looks for the sign of mercy in the sky;
Let Pestilence in all her horrors rise;
Where'er I turn, let Famine blast my eyes;
Let the earth yawn, and, ere they've time to think,
In the deep gulf let all my subjects sink
Before my eyes, whilst on the verge I reel;
Feeling, but as a monarch ought to feel,
Not for myself, but them, I'll kiss the rod,
And, having own'd the justice of my God,
Myself with firmness to the ruin give,
And die with those for whom I wish to live.

(*Gotham*, II, 297-314)

This passage is a "speaking" piece. Without knowing the context, one can easily imagine an actor declaiming it, with appropriate gestures, in the theatre. The high-pitched emotional tone, the appeals to the destructive forces of nature and to personifications of evil, the cues for dramatic gesture ("Where'er I turn," "before my eyes," "on the verge I reel," "I'll kiss the rod," etc.), the tempo mounting to a climax of death—all this is characteristic of a declamatory style more suitable on the stage than off. It is also a style not unlike that of Dryden (turgid and rhetorical) in many of his heroic plays. Actually, in context, the passage describes Churchill's violent reaction to the thought that a hated Stuart might become king of his utopian Gotham.

In the argumentative quality of his verse Churchill also resembles Dryden rather than Pope. Particularly in his satire—always a style of attack—Churchill strikes out to win through reason as well as abuse. And although sometimes his logic is faulty, it is rarely ineffective. In the following passage about the subservience of poets to patrons, he argues with the logic of "hence" and "therefore":

> Our real wants in a small compass lie;
> But lawless appetite, with eager eye,
> Kept in a constant fever, more requires,
> And we are burnt up with our own desires.
> Hence our dependence, hence our slavery springs;
> Bards, if contented, are as great as kings.
>
> .   .   .   .   .   .
>
> Chains were not forged more durable and strong
> For bards than others, but they've worn them long,
> And therefore wear them still; they've quite forgot
> What freedom is, and therefore prize her not . . .
>
> (*Independence*, 465-80)

Like his two famous predecessors in poetic satire, Churchill's chief weapon is the satiric portrait, the contemptuous "character." His method is usually that of caricature. Thus he attacks the actor-dramatist Arthur Murphy:

> Still in extremes, he knows no happy mean,
> Or raving mad, or stupidly serene.
> In cold-wrought scenes the lifeless actor flags,
> In passion, tears the passion into rags.
> Can none remember? Yes—I know all must—
> When in the Moor he ground his teeth to dust,
> When o'er the stage he Folly's standard bore,
> Whilst Common Sense stood trembling at the door.
>
> (*Rosciad*, 577-84)

This is intentional distortion in the manner of Dryden, from whom indeed the general idea and some of the phrases are taken (see the portrait of "Zimri" in *Absalom and Achitophel*). Pope's opposite tendency to ridicule by minimizing (see "Sporus": "this bug with gilded wings" in the *Epistle to Dr. Arbuthnot*) Churchill rarely uses.

Another noteworthy device in Churchill's satiric style is his use of words in unexpected contexts. Taking an ordinary word with a set of traditional meanings, he inverts or otherwise sharply changes the expected usage, thus giving the reader a start of surprise. Dryden often achieves this effect, as in the couplet:

> The rest to some faint meaning make pretense,
> But Shadwell never deviates into sense;

where "deviates *into* sense" provides the semantic shock. Similarly Churchill employs the device:

> They see not till they fall into the snares—
> Deluded into virtue unawares.
>
> (*Gotham*, II, 127-28)

> Their grateful country shall their fame record,
> And I myself descend to praise a lord.
>
> (*Candidate*, 103-4)

> Forth from the court, where sceptred sages sit,
> Abused with praise, and flatter'd into wit.
>
> (*Apology*, 37-38)

Less subtle but more characteristic of Churchill's contemptuous portraits are the series of scornful epithets which blast savagely in the manner of Juvenal, Dryden, and Johnson:

> Cold-blooded critics, by enervate sires
> Scarce hammer'd out when Nature's feeble fires
> Glimmer'd their last; whose sluggish blood, half froze,
> Creeps labouring through the veins, whose heart ne'er glows
> With fancy-kindled heat;—a servile race,
> Who, in mere want of fault all merit place;
> Who blind obedience pay to ancient schools,
> Bigots to Greece, and slaves to musty rules;
> With solemn consequence declared that none
> Could judge that cause but Sophocles alone:
> Dupes to their fancied excellence, the crowd,
> Obsequious to the sacred dictate, bow'd.
>
> (*Rosciad*, 179-90)

In all these epithets—"Cold-blooded," "enervate," "feeble," "sluggish," " servile," "blind," "slaves," "dupes," "obsequious," etc.—there is indeed insult piled upon injury!

The foregoing characteristics, generally speaking, place Churchill where he places himself and where his critics have placed him: in the tradition of satirists that comes down from Juvenal and Persius through Dryden to Johnson. This tradition produced satire which tends to be broad, violent, and rhetorical. It lacks the finesse, the sophistication, the well-mannered control, the subtlety of Horatian satire. To use a familiar critical comparison, it strikes with a bludgeon rather than a rapier. But there is another side of Churchill, a side which places him in the Horatian tradition as practiced by Pope and to which we may now turn.

The most obvious way in which Churchill failed to follow Dryden was his reluctance to use the triplet and the alexandrine, either together or separately. In the entire *Rosciad* (1090 lines), for example, there are no triplets and but two alexandrines (220 and 900); in *The Epistle to Hogarth*, none of either; in *The Apology*, one triplet (99-101); and elsewhere the situation is similar. If Churchill had modelled his style primarily on Dryden, it is remarkable that he should have rejected these devices, particularly since they would have given him more of the very thing he found most lacking in Pope—variety.

But it was in other ways, more characteristic of Pope, that Churchill achieved variety within the couplet. A study of his metric, syntax, and order of thought will reveal his relationship to this tradition. Such analysis will also reveal Churchill as a less careless and more disciplined artist than has been assumed. No hard and fast line can of course be drawn between Dryden and Pope; although many of the following characteristics may also be found in Dryden, they are all more typical of Pope. Like him Churchill almost invariably prefers monosyllabic rhyme words, and in both poets, therefore, the rhyme words are almost always masculine. Pope, for example, uses only three couplets with feminine endings in *The Rape of the Lock*, a poem of 794 lines. In *The Rosciad*, with 1090 lines, Churchill uses only two; in *The Epistle to Hogarth* (654 lines), none; and in *Gotham*, I (500 lines), one.[6]

As a means of achieving thought as well as metrical stress, Churchill prefers a verb for at least one of the rhyme words. In forty-nine of the first one hundred couplets of *The Rosciad*, one or both rhyme words are verbs; in fifty-six of the first one hundred couplets of *The Epistle to Hogarth*, one or both rhymes are verbs; and in the entire poem *Night* (191 couplets) the number is 103. This characteristic is one that Tillotson notes as remarkable in Pope.[7] Also like Pope, Churchill frequently divides verb and object by placing the one at the end of the first line and the other in the second.

---

[6] In these figures I do not include contractable two-syllable words, because inside the line Churchill usually contracts them.

[7] *Op. cit.*, p. 124.

This arrangement serves to tighten the unity of the couplet, for example:

> Reason, collected in herself, disdains
> The slavish yoke of arbitrary chains.
>
> (*Night*, 45-46)

> And bury meaning, save that we might spy
> Sense lowering on the penthouse of his eye.
>
> (*Independence*, 161-62)

The number and arrangement of stressed syllables within the line, of which the intricate system has been worked out for Pope, may be found essentially the same in Churchill. Following are examples of the four-, five-, and six-stress line:

> To make a secret of his vile amours.
>
> (*Times*, 292)

> And reach the heights which honest men despise.
>
> (*Rosciad*, 72)

> Did virtue move thee? No; 'twas pride, rank pride.
>
> (*Hogarth*, 393)

Churchill's usual practice, like that of his predecessors in the eighteenth century, is to vary these three types of line regularly, with four- and five-stress lines predominating. Thus the opening six lines of *The Epistle to Hogarth* scan as two fives, two fours, a six, and a four. In addition to these main types of line, three variations appear fairly often in Churchill and a fourth rarely: (a) the five-stress line with trochaic inversion, (b) the five-stress line with spondaic or pyrrhic substitution, (c) the three-stress line with two normal stresses suppressed, and (d) the alexandrine. Below are examples of these variations in their respective order:

> Shunning his steps, decrees, by honour taught.
>
> (*Author*, 286)

Joint judges were ordained to try the cause.

                                   (*Rosciad*, 230)

Who fashion'd without feelings, dost expect.

                                   (*Hogarth*, 177)

And all adown the stage in feeble murmurs dies.

                                   (*Rosciad*, 900)

Propriety of sound and sense was highly valued by Churchill, both in precept and practice. Sometimes he plays with onomatopoeia, like Pope in *An Essay on Criticism*, as when he mimics the verse of pseudo-poets who "make it all their business to describe":

> Let liquid gold emblaze the sun at noon,
> With borrow'd beams let silver pale the moon;
> Let surges hoarse lash the resounding shore,
> Let streams meander, and let torrents roar;
> Let them breed up the melancholy breeze
> To sigh with sighing, sob with sobbing trees.
>
>   (*Gotham*, II, 41-46)

And when criticizing other would-be poets who, "Railing at needful ornament depend On sense to bring them to their journey's end," he writes:

> They would not (Heaven forbid!) their course delay,
> Nor for a moment step out of the way,
> To make the barren road those graces wear
> Which Nature would, if pleased, have planted there.
>
>   (*Gotham*, II, 57-60)

The sound and rhythm of "Nor for a moment step out of the way" is perfect prose, and achieves its effect in context as well as Pope's more famous "And ten low words oft creep in one dull line."

Repetition of words within the line, which gives the effect

of an echo, is a favorite device of Churchill's; and the added emphasis on meaning makes the device a powerful one:

> Most lusciously declaims 'gainst luscious themes,
> And whilst he rails at blasphemy, blasphemes.
>
> (*Author*, 389-90)
>
> Peace to such men, if such men can have peace.
>
> (*Conference*, 73)
>
> A hag, who, loathing all, by all is loathed.
>
> (*Gotham*, I, 435)

A more complex and interesting kind of repetition, in which play on meaning is paramount, appears in the following instances:

> To coin newfangled wagers, and to lay 'em,
> Laying to lose, and losing not to pay 'em.
>
> (*Candidate*, 343-44)
>
> . . . thy great soul,
> Which pomps of this world never could control;
> Which never offer'd up at Power's vain shrine—
> Think not that pomp and power can work on mine.
>
> (*Warburton*, 29-32)

In the last example "pomp and power" ties the two previous lines to the third, provides a climax, and suddenly turns the thought from the person addressed (Bishop Warburton) to the author.

"Apt Alliteration's artful aid" Churchill constantly employs, despite his pretense to the contrary. In his satire it adds enormously to the tone of contempt and derision:

> With every pert, prim prettiness of youth.
>
> (*Journey*, 130)
>
> A smooth, smug stripling, in life's fairest prime.
>
> (*Times*, 421)
>
> No servile rules drew sickly taste aside,
> Secure he walk'd, for Nature was his guide.
>
> (*Apology*, 53-54)

Often the sounds are more subtly interchanged, as in the combination of *b* and *d* in the following line:

> And bless the donors for their daily bread:
> *(Prophesy,* 208)

or as below where, in the two adjective-noun phrases, the adjective of the first alliterates with the noun of the second:

> Where fiery zeal and Christian fury hung.
> *(Warburton,* 136)

Apart from metrical and sound effects, Churchill's versification consists chiefly of effects of balance within the line or couplet—balance in thought as well as syntax, for the two are inextricably related.   In Churchill, as in Pope and his close follower Gay, the simplest construction is the balanced line of two nouns and modifiers separated by a conjunction or preposition:

> Superior virtue and superior sense.
> *(Hogarth,* 3)

> The buskin'd heroes of the mimic stage.
> *(Rosciad,* 3)

Such lines usually have four stresses with the central accent suppressed.   Variety appears when a more important (and therefore stressed) word or phrase separates the balanced combinations:

> In full content he found the truest wealth.
> *(Gotham,* I, 57)

Here subject and verb separate them; in the following line it is the verb alone:

> By vilest means pursues the vilest ends.
> *(Rosciad,* 124)

Or the verb may appear at the beginning or at the end, still making it a five-stress line:

Urged the free dictates of an honest soul.
(*Hogarth*, 54)

And in full cry the eager hounds pursue.
(*Gotham*, I, 196)

Often the syntactic balance is accompanied by a contrast, instead of similarity, in the thought. In the following line "merit" and "bribes" are diametrically opposed in meaning, but they appear in a syntactic parallel:

Must add to force of merit, force of bribes.
(*Rosciad*, 18)

Similarly but with subtle variations:

Or, fond of knowledge, and averse from strife.
(*Hogarth*, 35)

Who talks of charity, but means a feast.
(*Gotham*, I, 34)

Should love of fame, in every noble mind
A brave disease, with love of virtue join'd.
(*Hogarth*, 31-32)

In the last couplet, the parallel-contrast appears near the beginning and near the end of the two lines, thus weaving them together.

In many other instances, Churchill (again like Pope and Gay) introduces elements that are out of balance or makes the balance one between unequal parts. In the following line, note the adjective–noun and adverb–verb combinations:

Vile interest scorn, nor madly grasp at power.
(*Hogarth*, 30)

The basic ideas are "scorn interest" and "grasp at power." Now when the poet begins by qualifying the first noun, we expect, if balance is to be maintained, that he will similarly qualify the second noun, "power"; instead he surprises us by qualifying not the noun but the second verb, "grasp." Another kind of unexpectedness occurs in the following line:

> Nor drawn by virtue's love from love of fame.
>
> (Gotham, I, 99)

Here the use of the inflected genitive ("virtue's love") sets up the expectancy of its repetition (i.e. "fame's love"), but instead we are given the periphrastic genitive ("love of fame"), a subtle variation.

When the balance is between two unequal parts, we naturally remark the word or phrase that makes them unequal. In the line,

> Renown'd in rhyme, revered for moral fame,
>
> (Hogarth, 142)

the balanced elements are "Renown'd in rhyme, revered for . . . fame." The adjective "moral" therefore provides the variation and attracts our attention. A somewhat subtler example appears in,

> Fiercer each snake, and sharper every dart,
>
> (Hogarth, 45)

where all is balanced except the extra syllable of "every" compared to its counterpart "each." A more intricate set of relationships may be seen in the couplet:

> And whilst she teaches, on vile interest's plan,
> As laws of God, the wild decrees of man.
>
> (Gotham, I, 85-86)

"Wild" in the second line is of course the unbalanced element, but in the couplet as a whole the phrases "on vile interest's plan" and "the wild decrees of man" are balanced and are made more emphatic by the presence of the rhyme words.

The reader's expectations are also pleasantly disturbed by variations in word order, a matter of pure syntax. The poet sets up a certain structure at the beginning of the line, and then reverses or otherwise changes it before the end:

> Pour seas of wine, and mountains raise of meat.
>
> (*Rosciad*, 24)

Here the structure of "Pour seas of wine" calls for its parallel "raise mountains of meat": we are given instead an inversion of verb and object. The phrases "of wine" and "of meat," however, maintain the opposite effect of perfect balance. Similarly in

> To her be granted, and denied to me,
>
> (*Gotham*, I, 106)

the perfectly balanced line would read: "To her be granted, and to me denied."

In the light of this discussion, it is clearly not the whole truth that "Churchill fled Pope for Dryden and Shakespeare,"[8] or that he "admired and followed Dryden rather than Pope."[9] These familiar critical statements are little more than half truths, supported indeed by the poet's own words (which are often intentional exaggerations), but contradicted by a critical examination of the poetry itself. It is true that Dryden was one of Churchill's models, and perhaps the one he most admired; but it is no less true that in important parts of his work Pope was the model.[10] The fact seems to be that Churchill rode both "coursers of ethereal race" in his brief but brilliant journey along the slopes of Parnassus, a journey that at times took him within seeing distance of the top.

II

Churchill's best work reveals him as a master craftsman and a poet who, within the neo-classic tradition, altered it by

---

[8] Van Doren, *op. cit.*, pp., 270-71.

[9] Oliver Elton, *A Survey of English Literature*, 1730-1780, I, 342.

[10] See also Edward H. Weatherly, "Churchill's Literary Indebtedness to Pope," *SP*, XLIII, 59-70.

certain technical achievements in the couplet form that were new or that were used in new ways by him. These achievements, however, did not flower until past the midpoint of his short career. Churchill's early poems ably continue the established tradition of heroic satire. *The Rosciad* is a series of biting portraits of contemporary actors and actresses, but there is nothing in it that Dryden had not done more brilliantly in *Absalom and Achitophel*. *The Apology* is also largely traditional, comparable in structure to the *Epistle to Dr. Arbuthnot*. The only notable change from *The Rosciad* is the increased use of irony—later to become the staple of Churchillian satire. The irony appears chiefly in lines 148-85, as part of the attack on critics and pastoral poets; but it lacks finish and subtlety. In *Night,* Churchill's third heroic satire, there is nothing new: on the whole it is an inferior performance.

More than a year later, however, appeared *The Prophecy of Famine,* in which Churchill struck the notes that were to characterize his mature work and his own contributions to heroic satire. In this poem irony, as a method of satire, becomes dominant, and lyrical overtones, based on the device of ironic eulogy, develop. The heroic couplet becomes freer and less limited to the epigrammatic norm. The sentence structure lengthens and becomes more involved, a change in syntax that vitally affects the versification. These developments are often crudely managed, but in extent and emphasis they are fresh and original achievements.

Structurally *The Prophecy of Famine* is divisible into three parts: an attack on the "simple" and "erudite" pastoral poem, an attack on the Scottish people in mock-heroic style, and an ironic pastoral about Scotland, which concludes with the prophecy by Famine. First a simple pastoral scene is presented with mock seriousness:

> Clad, as your nymphs were always clad of yore,
> In rustic weeds—a cook-maid now no more—

> Beneath an aged oak Lardella lies,
> Green moss her couch; her canopy the skies.
> From aromatic shrubs the roguish gale
> Steals young perfumes, and wafts them through the vale.
> The youth, turn'd swain, and skill'd in rustic lays,
> Fast by her side his amorous descant plays.
> Herds low, flocks bleat, pies chatter, ravens scream,
> And the full chorus dies a-down the stream.   (15-24)

The intentional archaisms ("rustic weeds," "swain," "rustic
lays," "a-down," etc.), the suggestion of "lard" in Lardella,
and the heaped-up collection of pastoral trappings make the
irony crudely obvious. Next the more presumptuous classical
pastoral is ridiculed:

> But when maturer Judgment takes the lead,
> These childish toys on Reason's altar bleed.
>
> .   .   .   .
>
> Then the rude Theocrite is ransack'd o'er,
> And courtly Maro call'd from Mincio's shore;
> Sicilian Muses on our mountains roam,
> Easy and free as if they were at home;
> Nymphs, Naiads, Nereids, Dryads, Satyrs, Fauns,
> Sport in our floods, and trip it o'er our lawns.   (29-52)

Then, after a mock deprecation of his own powers, which
make it impossible for him to aspire to writing pastorals, the
poet turns to Nature ("Thou, Nature, art my goddess . . .")
for the purpose of writing an heroic poem about Scotland:

> Of false refinements sick, and labour'd ease,
> Which art, too thinly veil'd, forbids to please,
> By Nature's charms (inglorious truth!) subdued,
> However plain her dress, and 'haviour rude,
> To northern climes my happier course I steer,
> Climes where the goddess reigns throughout the year;
> Where, undisturb'd by Art's rebellious plan,
> She rules the loyal laird, and faithful clan.   (103-10)

Although no clue to the irony is necessary, we are given one by the phrase "inglorious truth!" in the third line. A more complicated pattern of satire appears in the uses of "art" in the second and seventh lines. The meaning of the first one is directly satiric—"art, too thinly veil'd": the artificial claptrap of the pastoral conventions. The meaning of the second is ironic: "Art's rebellious plan" imposed upon Nature in Scotland would actually help by bringing order and beauty out of a chaos.

Next follows the mock-heroic praise of Scotland: "To that rare soil, where virtues clust'ring grow, What mighty blessings doth not England owe!"—

> Thence came the Ramsays, names of worthy note,
> Of whom one paints as well as t'other wrote;
> Thence, Home, disbanded from the sons of prayer
> For loving plays, though no dull dean was there;
> Thence issued forth, at great Macpherson's call,
> That old, new, epic pastoral, Fingal;
> Thence Malloch, friend alike of church and state,
> Of Christ and Liberty, by grateful Fate
> Raised to rewards, which, in a pious reign,
> All daring infidels should seek in vain;
> Thence simple bards, by simple prudence taught,
> To this wise town by simple patrons brought,
> In simple manner utter simple lays,
> And take, with simple pensions, simple praise. (125-38)

Two facts about this passage are noteworthy. The five-fold repetition of the "thence" construction illustrates a syntactic device that became one of the hallmarks of Churchill's, as it was of Johnson's, style. By means of this parallel series he was able, among other things, to enlarge the limits of the heroic couplet without resorting to full enjambment. The essential unity of the closed couplet is retained, but it is subordinated to and made a part of the larger verse paragraph. The last four lines of the passage illustrate another characteristic of Churchill's mature style: the repetition of single words with an intricate variation of meaning in context. Here the seven-fold repetition of "simple" conveys numerous meanings and shades of meanings, including those suggested by the shifts from direct satire to irony and back again.

Because this ironic attitude towards Scotland takes the form of eulogy, it enriches the satire by adding a strong lyrical note. The conspicuous example is of course the mock duet chanted by the two Scottish shepherds Jockey and Sawney (343-402). But even in the following couplets the lyrical quality is marked:

> Waft me, some muse, to Tweed's inspiring stream,
> Where all the little Loves and Graces dream;
> Where, slowly winding, the dull waters creep,
> And seem themselves to own the power of sleep.
>
> (139-42)

The music of the long *e* sounds here reinforces the lyrical "waft me where" thought and syntax. In a later passage, where the goddess Famine addresses the two shepherds, promising them England's riches (455-76), the repetition of a syntactic construction in series has the effect of a refrain, and thus induces a recurring lyricism.

The ironic praise of Scotland in the second part of the poem is interrupted by the voice of William Whitehead, the mediocre poet laureate:

> Presumptuous wretch! and shall a Muse like thine,
> An English Muse, the meanest of the nine,
> Attempt a theme like this?   (239-41)

to which the poet ironically submits ("Abash'd I heard, and with respect obey'd"). He then returns to the pastoral:

> From themes too lofty for a bard so mean,
> Discretion beckons to an humbler scene;

> The restless fever of ambition laid,
> Calm I retire, and seek the sylvan shade— (261-64)

and launches into elaborate mock-heroics, which constitute the concluding section of the poem (261-562). The two Scottish shepherds are presented living in complete squalor under the aegis of their goddess Famine. They bewail their woes in a mock-pastoral lament, after which the goddess appears and, in a long peroration, prophesies the exploitation of England for their benefit.

Except for the reappearance of certain characteristics of Churchill's maturing style, his next four poems—*An Epistle to William Hogarth*, *The Conference*, *The Author*, and *Gotham*—add little to his management of the heroic couplet. In the Hogarth poem irony appears, but in a minor key; and "Soul-soothing Panegyric's flowery way" is directly satirized instead of being made the medium of effective irony, as it is later in *The Candidate*. But the highly involved sentence structure, enlarging the norm of the heroic couplet, continues; and the device of parallel syntactic series is even more effectively employed, as in lines 165-72, 173-82, 183-212, and 401-8.

The Author acquires distinction for its series of brilliant vitriolic portraits, but they are in the traditional manner. The defense of authorship and the attacks on contemporary taste and pseudo-writers are comparable to similar developments in the *Epistle to Dr. Arbuthnot*. In fact, the opening couplet is a variation of Pope's more famous:

> Why did I write? what sin to me unknown
> Dipt me in ink, my parents', or my own?

What is more purely Churchill in this poem, however, is the use of parallel constructions in series and the terrific irony of the conclusion. There are two syntactic series, beginning at lines 51 and 93, of which the key elements are "Is this the land" and "How do I laugh." In context the first of these is repeated five times, the second four: the effect is a sweeping freedom of the heroic couplet and a powerful lyrical tone in both passages. The whole of *The Author* is direct satire until the very end. Then, after a stinging climactic portrait of John Kidgell, a minor writer and fashionable preacher, who,

> Most lusciously declaims 'gainst luscious themes,
> And whilst he rails at blasphemy, blasphemes,

the poet suddenly couples Kidgell and himself in a conclusion that is charged with irony:

> Such be their arts whom interest controls;
> Kidgell and I have free and modest souls:
> We scorn preferment which is gain'd by sin,
> And will, though poor without, have peace within.

About *The Conference* and *Gotham* less, for our purposes, need be said. *The Conference* is a rather carelessly written dialogue between Churchill and a Lord, in which the discussion answers the question, why the poet writes for the good of others instead of for the good of himself. In the argument the familiar Churchillian shibboleths are reviewed. The versification is, on the whole, commonplace.

Gotham is Churchill's longest poem in heroic couplets—perhaps its chief distinction. It pictures a kind of utopia, over which the poet rules as the ideal patriot king. In contrast to this picture, actual conditions of all kinds are attacked in direct generalized satire, from pseudo-poets to the Stuart pretender. If *The Apology* and *The Author* may in Churchill's career be compared to the *Epistle to Dr. Arbuthnot* in Pope's, then *Gotham* is Churchill's *Essay on Man*. Structurally *Gotham* is very weak, for its three books are little more than three separate poems. The first book is a kind of long discursive lyric with a six-line refrain that appears ten times throughout the poem. This striking device is not continued in Books II and III, which deal mainly with bad writers and the iniquities of the Stuart kings. In versification the heroic couplet comes nearest of anywhere in Churchill to breaking down. In the third book at least a quarter of the couplets are enjambed, creating an effect that in Churchill is weakening, for his control over his medium was often precarious. Furthermore, irony, one of Churchill's most powerful weapons, is inconspicuous in this poem.

It is in *The Candidate* that the full flavor and mature effect of Churchill's heroic satire first appear, although there are still crudities of style and weaknesses of construction. In fact, Churchill, who died at thirty-three and all of whose poetry was written in the last four years of his life, never lived to fulfill his promise: in one sense he is the Chatterton of neo-classic literature. But in *The Candidate* the lines of future development are clear: what he retained of the tradition and what he added may be evaluated from this poem.

Structurally *The Candidate* is divisible at the middle of its 806 lines. The first half is introductory and a general attack on the Earl of Sandwich; the second half deals with Sandwich's candidacy for the High Stewardship of Cambridge University. Within the first half there is a four-fold division: the poet's rejection of his former themes, his ironic appeal to "Panegyric," the ironic apostrophe to Sandwich, and the satiric portrait of Lothario, an ideal rake who is a "glorified" Sandwich. The last half of the poem is a self-contained unit, in which first Sandwich and then his henchmen at Cambridge are openly pilloried.

The first 178 lines show a remarkable use of the syntactic series which we have found so characteristic of Churchill. There are nine groups of couplets, each introduced by the "Enough of" construction and each introducing a former theme which is considered and then rejected. The themes, including ironically satire itself, are as follows: "Enough of Actors," "Enough of Authors," "Enough of Critics," "Enough of Scotland," "Enough of States," "Enough of

Patriots," "Enough of Wilkes," "Enough of Self," and "Enough of Satire." It is significant to note that by pretending to reject Satire, Churchill prepares the way for the ironic eulogy to which he turns next. First the eulogy is general—an ironic appeal to Panegyric in the thrice-repeated construction: "Come, Panegyric . . ." Then in answer to the question, "What patron shall I choose?" the selection is made in a three-fold exclamation, "Hail, Sandwich!" and the ironic eulogy to him begins. As it progresses, the method of attack shifts from irony to direct satire, back to irony, and again to direct satire—another characteristic of Churchill's style. Thus the Lothario portrait is direct satire, at the end of which the poet ingeniously prepares for the return to an ironic attack on Sandwich. Having created Lothario,

> . . . Nature, full of grace,
> Nor meaning birth and titles to be base,
> Made only one, and having made him, swore
> In mercy to mankind, to make no more:
> Nor stopp'd she there, but, like a generous friend,
> The ills which error caused, she strove to mend,
> And having brought Lothario forth to view,
> To save her credit, brought forth Sandwich too.
>
> (407-14)

Then as the poem proceeds the irony imperceptibly becomes outright satire until, in the second half, Sandwich and his friends are under direct attack.

Throughout *The Candidate* the syntax, thought, and versification develop qualities which are pure Churchill. Of these the most remarkable is the complexity of the relationship between syntax and versification.[11] One way in which this complexity is achieved is by means of syntactic series

---

[11] In Churchill's mature work there is "a new kind of feeling . . . deeply involved in the rhythms, especially in the relationship of syntax to versification. The long and involved sentence, with its numerous parenthetical interruptions, hesitations, and afterthoughts, is foreign to the other masters of the couplet": Winters, *op. cit.*, pp. 140-41.

within a larger series. Thus within the "Enough of Critics" passage occur the following lines (I have italicized the key words):

> What *though* they lay the realms of Genius waste,
> Fetter the fancy and debauch the taste;
> *Though* they, like doctors, to approve their skill,
> Consult not how to cure, but how to kill;
> *Though* by whim, envy, or resentment led,
> They damn those authors whom they never read;
> *Though*, other rules unknown, one rule they hold,
> To deal out so much praise for so much gold:
> *Though* Scot with Scot, in damned close intrigues,
> Against the commonwealth of letters leagues;
> Uncensured let them pilot at the helm,
> And rule in letters, as they ruled the realm.   (53-64)

This tightly knit structure enlarges the unit of the heroic couplet without breaking it down, and the rhythms become correspondingly freer.

Complication through parenthetical interruptions appears frequently. The following proportion of four parentheses in eight lines is not an extreme example:

> For me, (nor dare I lie) my leading aim
> (Conscience first satisfied) is love of fame;
> Some little fame derived from some brave few,
> Who prizing Honour, prize her votaries too.
> Let all (nor shall resentment flush my cheek)
> Who know me well, what they know, freely speak,
> So those (the greatest curse I meet below)
> Who know me not, may not pretend to know. (123-30)

Note too the repetition of words and phrases which suggest hesitations and afterthoughts: "love of fame; Some little fame . . . Who know me well, what they know . . . Who know me not, may not pretend to know," etc.

Churchill's very way of thinking was extremely complex,

a fact that has misled critics into assuming that his work is crude, rough, and careless. But in his better work the sentences, although highly involved, are not poorly constructed: on the contrary, they are surprisingly well built, considering their richness and complexity. The following passage is a case in point:

> Gods! with what joy, what honest joy of heart,
> Blunt as I am, and void of every art,
> Of every art which great ones in the state
> Practise on knaves they fear, and fools they hate,
> To titles with reluctance taught to bend,
> Nor prone to think that virtues can descend,
> Do I behold (a sight, alas! more rare
> Than honesty could wish) the noble wear
> His father's honours, when his life makes known
> They're his by virtue, not by birth alone.   (415-24)

The main thought of this sentence is: "Gods! with what joy . . . do I behold . . . the noble wear his father's honours . . . by virtue, not by birth alone." Yet this thought, expressed in nineteen words, is imbedded in a passage of eighty-two words!—a passage that makes use of the syntactic devices of exclamation, repetition, and parenthesis, as well as dependent clauses within one another.

Of Churchill's next four poems, two—*The Farewell* and *The Journey*—are distinctly inferior. Like *The Conference*, *The Farewell* is a dialogue, this time between the Poet and a Friend, on such general subjects as patriotism, philosophy, aristocrats, and poets. The satire is generalized and diluted, the versification weakened by too much enjambment. *The Journey* is autobiographical in a vague meandering sort of way; its satire is mild and general, with a lyrical overtone emphasized by the refrain-like couplet:

> Let them their appetite for laughter feed;
> I on my Journey all alone proceed . . .

In both poems the satire is, for the most part, direct; irony is inconspicuous.

Independence is an attack on patrons, stiffly and mechanically presented through the device of a trial, in which the case for the patron and the case for the poet are argued in the court of Reason. The poet is obviously Churchill and the Lord a satiric type-portrait. Manly independence, the theme of the poem, can exist only when aristocratic patrons are rejected *à la* Churchill. In all this there is nothing new, and certainly nothing to compare in devastating effect with Johnson's prose letter to Chesterfield on the same subject.

The Times represents a return to a more specific subject for satire: public immorality as seen in a series of particular evils in particular people or types of people. The more tightly controlled versification reappears, along with many of the other more effective characteristics of Churchill's style. But especially in structure *The Times* is not up to the level of *The Candidate* or even, for that matter, of *The Prophecy of Famine*.

One more poem by Churchill remains to be considered: the *Fragment of a Dedication to Dr. W. Warburton, Bishop of Gloucester*. Probably this unfinished satire was the last that Churchill wrote; certainly, all things considered, it contains his best poetry. The device of a formal dedication was perfectly suited to Churchill's peculiar talent for "profound and bitter innuendo." He had employed ironic eulogy before, especially in *The Prophecy of Famine* and *The Candidate*; but the form of the dedication is the medium for eulogy *par excellence*. When it is used as the vehicle for subtle and sustained irony, the effect is comparable to that of the mock-heroic at its best.

Although it is unfinished, the *Dedication* forms a structural unit which may be divided into three parts. The first seventy-two lines introduce the subject and give the reasons why the poet admires Warburton, ending with the summary:

> Thy virtue, not thy rank, demands my lays;
> 'Tis not the Bishop, but the Saint, I praise:
> Raised by that theme, I soar on wings more strong,
> And burst forth into praise withheld too long.

The next forty lines describe the assistance that Churchill had hoped to get from him:

> Much did I wish, though little could I hope,
> A friend in him who was the friend of Pope.

And the last sixty-eight lines deal with the futility of that hope, because Warburton had more important things to do than "waste his precious time, On which so much depended, for a rhyme."

All the characteristics of Churchill's mature style appear fully developed in the *Dedication*. Thus the poem opens with a thrice-repeated "Health to great Glo'ster," which binds together the first twenty-eight lines. Then there follow two series of parallel constructions, describing what it is not, and what it is, that the poet admires in Warburton (33-72). The highly involved syntax and thought complications continue throughout the poem, as, for example, in the following passage:

> Much did I wish, e'en whilst I kept those sheep
> Which, for my curse, I was ordain'd to keep,
> Ordain'd, alas! to keep through need, not choice,
> Those sheep which never heard their shepherd's voice;
> Which did not know, yet would not learn their way;
> Which stray'd themselves, yet grieved that I should stray;
> Those sheep which my good father (on his bier
> Let filial duty drop the pious tear)
> Kept well, yet starved himself; e'en at that time
> Whilst I was pure and innocent of rhyme;
> Whilst, sacred dulness ever in my view,
> Sleep at my bidding crept from pew to pew,
> Much did I wish, though little could I hope,
> A friend in him who was the friend of Pope.   (73-86)

In the above sentence of 122 words, only the last couplet of nineteen words expresses the main idea; the rest is dependent, digressive, and contributory. Yet the entire passage is unified by devices typical of Churchill: the "Much did I wish" clause of the first line repeated in the next to the last; the repetition of the "which," the "whilst," and the "those sheep which" clauses; and the single enjambed couplet (7-8) carefully embedded in the center of the passage.

Lyrical qualities are more marked than ever in the *Dedication*. They arise chiefly out of four characteristics of the poem: (1) syntactic repetition with the effect of a refrain, (2) the constant intrusion of the personal note, (3) the rhetorical device of exclamations, and (4) the use of a non-epigrammatic norm for the heroic couplet, which creates larger rhythms and a more lyrical swing. Often the lyrical quality is generally implicit in the music and meaning:

> Raised by that theme, I soar on wings more strong,
> And burst forth into praise withheld too long. (71-72)

> O glorious man! thy zeal I must commend,
> Though it deprived me of my dearest friend. (145-46)

One of the most striking effects of the *Dedication* comes from the poet's unusual preoccupation with himself throughout the poem. This personal note creates a lyrical atmosphere, the effect of which is comparable to Donne's achievements in the satirical lyric. The result is an enormous increase in richness and complexity. There is, for example, a remarkable fusion of opposites in which the poet himself is treated sympathetically and Warburton is seemingly treated likewise, but actually is bitterly attacked. This juxtaposition of author and subject appears from the beginning:

> Health to great Glo'ster—nor, through love of ease,
> Which all priests love, let this address displease. (11-12)

The hint of satire here is complicated by the fact that, two lines above, Churchill had written:

> Truth best becomes an orthodox divine,
> And, spite of hell, that character is mine.

Thus the "love of ease, Which all priests love" doubles back and includes the poet as well as his victim, for both are or were "priests." The reader then must see that the satiric thrust aimed at Warburton is direct and the one at the author ironic. Also at the end of the poem:

> Let him not, gorged with power, and drunk with state,
> Forget what once he was, though now so high;
> How low, how mean, and full as poor as I.

The personal comparison provides an intricate intermingling of methods: the epithets "low," "mean," and "poor" apply directly to Warburton, but ironically to Churchill. And along with these complexities the unmixed irony of most of the lines continues, making the whole texture extremely rich.

In the poem as a whole the tensions set up between the contrasting attitudes of irony and eulogy create "a number of feelings belonging neither to irony nor to eulogy, but capable of joining with both."[12] Out of context the subtlety and complexity of these interplays of thought and feeling can only be suggested. They appear most clearly in the succession of hints at the ironic nature of the eulogy. These vary from the most subtle early in the poem to an outright attack on Warburton at the end. Thus Churchill writes about bishops' mitres:

> . . . mitres, which shine
> So bright in other eyes, are dull in mine,
> Unless set off by virtue.   (39-41)

The qualification may or may not apply to Warburton; the hint is there, but that is all. Again about the man himself:

> . . . and through thy skin
> Peeps out that courtesy which dwells within. (53-54)

---

[12] Winters, *op. cit.*, p. 140.

"Peeps out"—is this a sly dig? The next is more certain:

> But what is birth, when, to delight mankind,
> Heralds can make those arms they cannot find;
> When thou art to thyself, thy sire unknown,
> A whole Welsh genealogy alone?   (57-60)

Later the hints become broader and progressively more damaging:

> His judgment teach me, from the critic school,
> How not to err, and how to err by rule.   (91-92)

> But you, my lord, renounced attorneyship
> With better purpose, and more noble aim,
> And wisely play'd a more substantial game. (158-60)

>   . . . despise not one
> For want of smooth hypocrisy undone.   (167-68)

Until, at the conclusion of the poem, all pretense is dropped, and the satire becomes a direct attack.

In method of attack the *Dedication* is closest to that of Pope in *The First Epistle of the Second Book of Horace: To Augustus*. Pope's use of ironic eulogy, particularly at the beginning and end of his satire, is directly comparable to Churchill's. Thus Churchill's ironic explanation of Warburton's neglect of his poetry:

>   . . . could I believe
> That he, the servant of his Maker sworn,
> The servant of his Saviour, would be torn
> From their embrace, and leave that dear employ,
> The cure of souls, his duty and his joy,
> For toys like mine, and waste his precious time,
> On which so much depended, for a rhyme? (114-20)

parallels Pope's similar idea about George II:

> How shall the Muse, from such a monarch steal
> An hour, and not defraud the Public Weal?   (5-6)

But, unlike the *Dedication*, the epistle *To Augustus* is not predominantly ironic, so the total effect is quite different. Furthermore, the heroic couplet norm in Pope remains epigrammatic; in Churchill it is something else. The difference may be suggested in such a passage as the following:

> I ask no favour; not one *note* I crave;
> And when this busy brain rests in the grave,
> (For till that time it never can have rest)
> I will not trouble you with one bequest.   (13-16)

Here, without resorting to full enjambment, Churchill uses a couplet that permits the fusing of the four lines into a unit; yet the first couplet, although syntactically divided, is unified by the life-death thought contrast.   More importantly this couplet retains a rhythmic identity because of the parenthetical interruption that follows it: the parenthesis stops the tendency of the thought to run on, thereby increasing our awareness of the couplet unity.   Churchill often employs other kinds of hesitations, 'repetitions, and afterthoughts in this way—as safeguards against the collapse of the couplet into run-on verse paragraphs: for example,

> Far, far be that from thee—yes, far from thee
> Be such revolt from grace, and far from me
> The will to think it—guilt is in the thought.
> Not so, not so hath Warburton been taught,
> Not so learn'd Christ—recall that day, well known,
> When (to maintain God's honour—and his own)
> He call'd blasphemers forth: methinks I now
> See stern rebuke enthroned on his brow,
> And arm'd with tenfold terrors . . .   (127-35)

The effect of this couplet style is different from Pope's; yet it is far more different from the enjambed couplet of, for example, Shelley's *Epipsychidion*.

Few, if any, of Churchill's couplets are memorable out of context.   Probably his best-known line is the second of a couplet from *The Prophecy of Famine*, where he refers to himself:

> Who often, but without success, have pray'd
> For apt Alliteration's artful aid . . .   (85-86)

And even this line, in a modern anthology, has been attributed to Pope! Nevertheless Churchill's couplets retain their identity within the larger unit, of which they are the basis. They remain the pattern which is never obliterated, no matter how far the variations may digress.

The basic norm of Churchill's versification is the non-epigrammatic heroic couplet; the basic norm of his satire is irony. And for powerful and sustained irony the *Dedication to Dr. W. Warburton* is unequalled in English verse satire. Its only peer is in prose: Swift's *Modest Proposal*. The *Dedication* is also, as we have seen, Churchill's finest neo-classic poem. At his best—in this poem and in parts of *The Prophecy of Famine*, *The Author*, and *The Candidate*—Churchill is one of the masters of the couplet and the last great neo-classic satirist.

Chapter V

Young and Cowper:
The Neo-Classicist *Malgré Lui*

AFTER Pope, Johnson and Churchill are the real masters of satire in heroic-couplet form. The record, however, would be incomplete without a brief consideration of two other poets whose reputations lie in other directions, but who also tried their hands at this kind of verse. Both Edward Young and William Cowper established themselves as poets by publishing satires—Young in the manner of Pope, Cowper in the manner of Dryden and Churchill; and Young was personally acquainted with Pope, as was Cowper with Churchill.

I

Young wrote a great many more heroic-couplet poems than is usually realized, two-fifths of his nondramatic work being in this form. But quantity is higher than quality in these poems, so the world is no doubt right in preferring even the loose and lurid blank verse of *Night Thoughts* to most of them, particularly such inept and mechanical effusions as *The Last Day* and *The Force of Religion*. Nor are the excessively laudatory epistles to Addison, Tickell, Lord Landsdowne, and Sir Robert Walpole much better.

The seven satires, collectively entitled *Love of Fame, the Universal Passion*, and the two epistles to Pope are Young's best poems in heroic couplets; and, as we shall see, even they are by no means equal in merit. Five of the satires are directed at men, two at women (the fifth and sixth). In them all, Young's procedure is a combination of moral and satiric editorializing interspersed between satiric type-portraits. Structurally this method tends to lack unity and to be too mechanical. The following passage from the first satire illustrates these techniques:

> When men of infamy to grandeur soar,
> They light a torch to show their shame the more.
> Those governments which curb not evils, cause!
> And a rich knave's a libel on our laws.
>
> Belus with solid glory will be crown'd;
> He buys no phantom, no vain empty sound;
> But builds himself a name; and, to be great,
> Sinks in a quarry an immense estate!
> In cost and grandeur, Chandos he'll outdo;
> And Burlington, thy taste is not so true.
> The pile is finish'd! ev'ry toil is past;
> And full perfection is arriv'd at last;
> When, lo! my lord to some small corner runs,
> And leaves state-rooms to strangers and to duns.
>
> The man who builds, and wants wherewith to pay,
> Provides a home from which to run away.
> In Britain, what is many a lordly seat,
> But a discharge in full for an estate?[1]

The satiric portrait of ten lines is embedded in a framework of two four-line units of generalized moral comment. The arrangement is mechanical and heavy-handed. "Belus" is a man of "infamy" who obviously lacked the "wherewith to pay." So what? we ask, and are not impressed, because Belus is a straw figure. Furthermore, his weakness (ostentatious display of wealth) fails to materialize: there are no vivid details picturing his palace—it remains a "pile." Logical unity is at least strained in this passage when we consider in context the assertion, "Those governments which curb not evils, cause! And a rich knave's a libel on our laws." Belus

---

[1] *The Poetical Works of Edward Young,* ed. J. Mitford, II, 69: all references to Young's work are to this edition.

is a rich knave who brings about his own downfall: why there-fore should the government curb him and why is he "a libel on our laws"?

Young is overfond of another device that tends to weaken the structural unity of his poems: the epigrammatic couplet. Too often "single couplets sparkle with a brilliancy and point, that concentrates the allusion or image within their narrow bounds, and separates it from the rest of the poem."[2] In most of the satires (particularly the second and third), the result is a hodgepodge of mediocre and brilliant fragments. This fondness for epigram also leads Young into illogicalities that further weaken unity within the poems. Consider, for example, the opening verse paragraph of the third satire, dedicated "to the right honourable Mr. Dodington":

> Long, Dodington, in debt, I long have sought
> To ease the burthen of my grateful thought;
> And now a poet's gratitude you see;
> Grant him two favours, and he'll ask for three:
> For whose the present glory, or the gain?
> You give protection, I a worthless strain.
> You love and feel the poet's sacred flame,
> And know the basis of a solid fame;
> Tho' prone to like, yet cautious to commend,
> You read with all the malice of a friend;
> Nor favour my attempts that way alone,
> But, more to raise my verse, conceal your own.

> (II, p. 84)

The witty punch line appears in the fifth couplet: "You read with all the malice of a friend." The rest of the passage establishes the traditional idea of the poet's inferiority to his patron, with repeated implications of abject praise. With this context the tone and meaning of "the malice of a friend" are out of keeping. In itself the phrase is witty, ironic, and perhaps intentionally ambiguous; but in context it enforces two alternatives, either of which must constitute a blemish

---

[2] *Young*, ed. J. Mitford, I, xxviii.

on the passage: the author is insincere in his praise or he does not mean what he says in this line.

The most obvious weakness in structure in Young's satires arises from the simple fact of his being unable to stick to the subject. Most of these poems reveal a woolgathering tendency (by no means absent from *Night Thoughts* as well!) to meander from one subject to another and back again. Thus in the second satire Young introduces "Codrus," a lover of books for their expensive bindings—

> The gaudy shelves with crimson bindings glow,
> And Epictetus is a perfect beau . . .   (II, p. 76)

This suggests the next portrait, that of "Lorenzo":

> On buying books Lorenzo long was bent,
> But found at length that it reduc'd his rent.

Lorenzo goes broke, however, after which we wind back to another aspect of Codrus' folly:

> Not in his authors' liveries alone
> Is Codrus' erudite ambition shown:
> Editions various, at high prices bought,
> Inform the world what Codrus would be thought;
> And to his cost another must succeed
> To pay a sage, who says that he can read;
> Who titles knows, and indexes has seen;
> But leaves to Chesterfield what lies between.
>   (II, pp. 76-77)

When this kind of thing occurs too often in Young's poems, we may be forgiven for answering the rhetorical questions in his following couplet with an emphatic "yes" and "no" respectively:

> But wanders not my satire from my theme?
> Is this too owing to the love of fame?   (II, p. 141)

Our discussion of Young's fondness for epigram suggests the technical basis for his heroic couplet. It is the strictest form of the couplet, the one established by Pope: the epi-grammatic norm. Young's satires are replete with excellent examples, some witty, some moralistic, all sententious, as in the following description of a time for satire:

> When churchmen scripture for the classics quit,
> Polite apostates from God's grace to wit;
> When men grow great from their revenue spent,
> And fly from bailiffs into parliament;
> When dying sinners, to blot out their score,
> Bequeath the church the leavings of a whore . . .
>
> (II, p. 64)

Or the following pictures of people:

> Is there a tongue, like Delia's o'er her cup,
> That runs for ages without winding up?   (II, p. 73)

> The fame men give is for the joy they find;
> Dull is the jester, when the joke's unkind.   (II, p. 78)

> What then is to be done? Be wise with speed;
> A fool at forty is a fool indeed.   (II, p. 83)

> When Britain calls, th' embroider'd patriots run,
> And serve their country—if the dance is done.
>
> (II, p. 91)

> As sure as cards, he to th' assembly comes,
> And is the furniture of drawing-rooms.   (II, p. 96)

> This truth sagacious Lintot knows so well,
> He starves his authors, that their works may sell.
>
> (II, p. 100)

> She reads the psalms and chapters for the day,
> In—Cleopatra, or the last new play.   (II, p. 104)

In all these couplets the Pope formula appears with a ven-geance: completion of the thought with the couplet, parallel syntax (in the first passage), emphatic masculine rhymes, caesura after the fourth, fifth, or sixth syllable (with two exceptions), and four or five stresses to the line.

In fact, this very adherence to the Pope formula is a source of weakness in Young's handling of the couplet: he adheres so closely that he misses a more important axiom of Pope's, to "snatch a grace beyond the reach of art." This lack of metrical and syntactic variety in Young's work is unfortunately too often combined with an intellectual pedestrianism that places his heroic-couplet poems among those of the second order, if not worse. In the following typical passage from the fifth satire "On Women," we may in miniature assess these values:

> Wine may indeed excite the meekest dame;
> But keen Xantippe, scorning borrow'd flame,
> Can vent her thunders, and her lightnings play,
> O'er cooling gruel, and composing tea:
> Nor rest by night, but, more sincere than nice,
> She shakes the curtains with her kind advice:
> Doubly, like echo, sound is her delight,
> And the last word is her eternal right.
> Is 't not enough, plagues, wars, and famines rise
> To lash our crimes, but must our wives be wise?
>
> (II, p. 105)

Within the Pope formula this passage is reasonably well varied. There are, for example, substitutions in the first metrical foot of three lines; five caesuras after the fifth syllable, four after the fourth, and one after the sixth; and five four-stress lines, four five-stress, and one six-stress. What variation there is, however, is insufficient to lighten the unleavened thought and heavy-handed expression. The effect of wine as "borrow'd flame" is none too happy an image; Xantippe's thunders and lightnings are trite ones; and the phrase "composing tea" is in context inept and awkward. Shaking the curtain with her kind advice is no better, and the couplet "Doubly, like echo, sound is her delight, And the last word is her eternal right" is not only trite but vague in its use of "Doubly." Finally, the last couplet is an overstrained attempt at witty epigrammatic climax.

As we noted in the discussion of "dramatic tension" in the work of Dryden, Pope, Johnson, and Churchill, contrast is an essential characteristic of satire. In the satires of Young, however, there is a lack of dramatic tension because the contrasts are static: they remain black and white, with no lights and shadows. He also deals too exclusively in extremes which tend to give his satires a mechanical unreality. Consider, for example, the attack on female hypochondriacs:

> Lemira's sick; make haste; the doctor call:
> He comes; but where's his patient? At the ball.
> The doctor stares; her woman curtsies low,
> And cries, "My lady, Sir, is always so:
> Diversions put her maladies to flight:
> True, she can't stand, but she can dance all night:
> I've known my lady (for she loves a tune)
> For fevers take an opera in June:
> And, tho' perhaps you'll think the practice bold,
> A midnight park is sov'reign for a cold:
> With cholics, breakfasts of green fruit agree;
> With indigestions, supper just at three."
> A strange alternative, replies Sir Hans,
> Must women have a doctor, or a dance?
> Though sick to death, abroad they safely roam,
> But droop and die, in perfect health, at home:
> For want—but not of health, are ladies ill;
> And tickets cure beyond the doctor's pill.

> (II, pp. 108-9)

Not only are the contrasts unrelieved extremes, but there are too many of them: the total effect is overdone. There is reason for the maid's recital of her mistress's ailments and remedies, but the doctor's comment beyond the first couplet (lines 13-14) is an act of supererogation: the last two couplets are unnecessary and constitute a blemish on the passage.

In structure and technical achievements, Young's best poem as a whole is probably the sixth satire "On Women." It has a well-marked introduction (the first twenty lines) and conclusion (the last twenty-eight lines), between which are a group of twenty major satiric portraits of typical women and many passages of satiric and moral comment by the author. His purpose, with emphasis upon the idea of a portrait gallery, appears clearly in the introduction:

> Ye fair! to draw your excellence at length,
> Exceeds the narrow bounds of human strength;
> You, here, in miniature your picture see;
> Nor hope from Zincks more justice than from me.
> My portraits grace your mind, as his your side;
> His portraits will inflame, mine quench, your pride.
> He's dear, you frugal; choose my cheaper lay;
> And be your reformation all my pay.   (II, p. 123)

The poem has a more ingenious and effective beginning than is usual with Young. The device of interweaving dedicatory compliment with witty satire on patronage sets a satisfactory tone for the entire poem;

> I sought a patroness, but sought in vain.
> Apollo whisper'd in my ear—"Germain."—
> I know her not.—"Your reason's somewhat odd;
> Who knows his patron, now?" replied the god.
> "Men write, to me, and to the world, unknown;
> Then steal great names, to shield them from the town."

The portraits follow no prescribed form, except that each one stresses a different set of weaknesses. Thus "Lavinia is polite, but not profane; To church as constant as to Drury Lane . . . Amasia hates a prude, and scorns restraint; Whate'er she is, she'll not appear a saint . . . Lucia thinks happiness consists in state; She weds an idiot, but she eats on plate . . . Mira, endow'd with every charm to bless, Has no design, but on her husband's peace . . . Brunetta's wise in actions great,

and rare; But scorns on trifles to bestow her care . . . Fair
Isabella is so fond of fame, That her dear self is her eternal
theme," etc. They appear either in succession, or the series
is interrupted by more generalized satire or moralizing. Of
the second procedure, the portrait of "Cleora" is typical:

> Of rank and riches proud, Cleora frowns;
> For are not coronets akin to crowns?
> Her greedy eye, and her sublime address,
> The height of avarice and pride confess.
> You seek perfections worthy of her rank;
> Go, seek for her perfections at the bank.
> By wealth unquench'd, by reason uncontrol'd,
> For ever burns her sacred thirst of gold.
> As fond of five-pence, as the veriest cit;
> And quite as much detested as a wit.
>   Can gold calm passion, or make reason shine?
> Can gold dig peace, or wisdom, from the mine?
> Wisdom to gold prefer; for 'tis much less
> To make our fortune, than our happiness . . .
>   (II, p. 132)

And so on for thirty-six more lines on the same theme, which,
as we noted in an earlier context, is too much editorializing
on one portrait.

In this poem, as in all of Young's heroic couplets, there
is generally a lack of subtlety and, more important, an absence
of neo-classic "wit," the illustration of which may be seen
in the juxtaposition of comparable passages from Young and
Dryden:

> Syrena is for ever in extremes,
> And with a vengeance she commends, or blames.
> Conscious of her discernment, which is good,
> She strains too much to make it understood.
> Her judgment just, her sentence is too strong;
> Because she's right, she's ever in the wrong. (II, p. 129)

> Railing and praising were his usual themes,

And both, to show his judgment, in extremes:
So over violent, or over civil,
That every man with him was God or Devil.
In squand'ring wealth was his peculiar art:
Nothing went unrewarded, but desart . . .

(*Absalom and Achitophel*, I, 304-9)

As extremists Syrena and Zimri (the Duke of Bucking-
ham) have a common bias, and of the two Syrena is less
one-sided. But, except for the paradox in the last line, her
portrait is obvious and pedestrian. In Dryden, on the other
hand, the irony of "to show his judgment" infuses life into
the matter-of-fact statement of the first couplet. Similarly
the reversal of expected meaning in the last line contributes
the element of surprise that is one ingredient in the "wit" of
this kind of verse. At best Young manages a heavy-handed
kind of wit in this manner, in such a passage as the following:

The love of gaming is the worst of ills;
With ceaseless storms the blacken'd soul it fills;
Inveighs at heaven, neglects the ties of blood;
Destroys the power and will of doing good;
Kills health, pawns honour, plunges in disgrace,
And, what is still more dreadful—spoils your face.

(II, p. 139)

Judging by the meaning of the words in this passage, it
should be powerful satire; but something is lacking: the
spirit, the over-all tone, does not measure up to the high
satiric purpose. Swift is said to have remarked about Young's
satire in general, that it should be more angry or more merry.

As satire and as neo-classic poetry, there are passages in
Young's two epistles to Pope which represent his most mature
work and which are superior to anything in the seven formal
satires. The first of these two poems (published in 1730)
deals with "the authors of the age," and is similar to one
aspect of the *Epistle to Dr. Arbuthnot:* the attack on pseudo-

writers. Early in the poem Young's assertion that his "tor-
mented ear Less dreads a pillory than a pamphleteer" is fol-
lowed later by his statement of purpose:

> Shall we not censure all the motley train,
> Whether with ale irriguous, or champaign?

Like the formal satires, this poem is a combination of satiric
portraits and more generalized attack. Typical is the por-
trait of "Lico," part of which follows:

> Thus having reason'd with consummate skill,
> In immortality he dips his quill:
> And, since blank paper is denied the press,
> He mingles the whole alphabet by guess:
> In various sets, which various words compose,
> Of which, he hopes, mankind the meaning knows.
>
> (II, p. 340)

The ironic wit of the first couplet and the satiric humor of
the others combine to make the passage strikingly effective.

A somewhat later passage is equally successful and tech-
nically more interesting—part of the portrait of "Clodio":

> Clodio for bread his indolence must quit,
> Or turn a soldier, or commence a wit.
> Such heroes have we! all, but life, they stake;
> How must Spain tremble, and the German shake!
> Such writers have we! all, but sense, they print;
> Ev'n George's praise is dated from the mint.
> In arms contemptible, in arts profane,
> Such swords, such pens, disgrace a monarch's reign.
> Reform your lives before you thus aspire,
> And steal (for you can steal) celestial fire.
>
> (II, p. 341)

The use of parallel syntax and structural repetition makes this
passage unusually well unified. Clodio must become either
a soldier or a writer: the remainder of the passage deals in
an equal and balanced way with these two subjects. The

two are united in the fourth couplet; the fifth and last is appropriately the climax that includes all that has gone before. And, of equal importance, it provides an unexpected shock in the double meaning of "steal (for you can steal)" in context.

Young's second epistle to Pope is much less satiric and spectacular because of its subject:

> Meanwhile, O friend! indulge me, if I give
> Some needful precepts how to write, and live!

After observing about the name of author, "How few deserve it, and what numbers claim!" Young proceeds to write a kind of "conjectures on original composition" in verse. For our purposes one sample of his procedure will suffice:

> Let nature art, and judgment wit, exceed;
> O'er learning reason reign; o'er that, your creed:
> Thus virtue's seeds, at once, and laurel's grow;
> Do thus, and rise a Pope, or a Despreau:
> And when your genius exquisitely shines,
> Live up to the full lustre of your lines:
> Parts but expose those men who virtue quit;
> A fallen angel is a fallen wit;
> And they plead Lucifer's detested cause,
> Who for bare talents challenge our applause (II, p. 355)

In traditional couplets this is an adequate treatment of the familiar thesis that literature is "at bottom a criticism of life."

Compared to Johnson, Churchill, and even Gay, Young must be placed among the second order of neo-classic satirists. That he considered himself inferior at least to Pope is implied in the appeal with which he introduced his seven satires:

> Why slumbers Pope, who leads the tuneful train,
> Nor hears that virtue, which he loves, complain?

Anyone who in 1725 (after the publication of the *Essay on Criticism* and *The Rape of the Lock*) could refer to Pope as one "who leads the tuneful train" would not be likely to become a major satirist himself.

II

Cowper was also a prolific composer of heroic couplets: among his miscellaneous poems in this form, he wrote tales and fables, descriptions, epistles, epitaphs, and "lines." But his major work in couplets is the group of eight satires and didactic poems with which he began his poetic career: "Table Talk," "The Progress of Error," "Truth," "Expostulation," "Hope," "Charity," "Conversation," and "Retirement," to which should be added the later "Tirocinium, A Review of Schools." Of these the most interesting, technically and in subject matter, are "Table Talk," "Conversation," and "Retirement." They contain most of his satire and much of that sympathetic description of the commonplaces of life and nature for which he is better known in his blank verse. The other couplet poems, for the most part, not only reveal nothing new in the handling of the form, but are too solemnly and monotonously moralistic.

Compared to the couplets of Young, those of Cowper are generally freer and more "relaxed." Written as they were in the last twenty years of the eighteenth century, they anticipate the couplet style of the succeeding generation rather than maintain the strict heroic couplet of Pope and Johnson. In this respect Cowper is closer to the Churchill of *Gotham* than he is to his boyhood friend's stronger major satires, such as *The Prophecy of Famine, The Candidate,* and the *Dedication to Warburton.* Although Cowper's own couplets are broadly within the neo-classic tradition, his critical view of the heroic couplet, as expressed in his letters and poetry, is strikingly similar to that of Keats and Leigh Hunt in their campaign against this poetic form later. Considering that he wrote so many couplet poems, it is rather surprising to find Cowper commenting as follows:

Long before I thought of commencing poet myself, I have com-
plained and heard others complain of the wearisomeness of such
poems. Not that I suppose that tedium the effect of rhyme
itself, but rather of the perpetual recurrence of the same pause
and cadence, unavoidable in the English couplet.[3]

And in "Table Talk," his first heroic-couplet poem, Cowper
levels these strictures specifically at Pope:

> But he (his musical finesse was such
> So nice his ear, so delicate his touch)
> Made poetry a mere mechanic art;
> And ev'ry warbler has his tune by heart.
>
> (652-55)[4]

In contrast to Cowper's assertion that monotony is "unavoid-
able in the English couplet," he here uses a variation that is
also characteristic of Churchill: the parenthesis which, with-
out resorting to full enjambment, unifies the two couplets.

The frequency and regularity of this device in Cowper's
work makes it, in fact, one of his most striking variations
from the typical heroic couplet. The formula is indicated
in the lines on Pope above: the parenthesis takes up a line
and a half or more of the couplet, leaving the non-paren-
thetic beginning to be grammatically completed in the couplet
that follows:

> Sing, muse, (if such a theme, so dark, so long,
> May find a muse to grace it with a song)
> By what unseen and unsuspected arts
> The serpent error twines round human hearts.
>
> ("Progress of Error," 1-4)

> The truth is (if the truth may suit your ear,
> And prejudice have left a passage clear)
> Pride has attain'd its most luxuriant growth,
> And poison'd ev'ry virtue in them both.
>
> ("Truth," 113-16)

[3] *William Cowper's Letters, A Selection*, ed. E. V. Lucas, p. 438.
[4] *The Poetical Works of William Cowper*, ed. H. S. Milford: all references
to Cowper's poems are to this edition.

> Say not (and, if the thought of such defence
> Should spring within thy bosom, drive it thence)
> What nation amongst all my foes is free
> From crimes as base as any charg'd on me?
>
> ("Expostulation," 708-11)

> Leuconomus (beneath well-sounding Greek
> I slur a name a poet must not speak)
> Stood pilloried on infamy's high stage,
> And bore the pelting scorn of half an age.
>
> ("Hope," 554-57)

> Suppose (when thought is warm, and fancy flows,
> What will not argument sometimes suppose?)
> An isle possess'd by creatures of our kind,
> Endu'd with reason, yet by nature blind.
>
> ("Charity," 379-82)

In other ways, however, Cowper relaxes the couplet more freely. One of these is his relatively frequent use of the triplet:

> And, of all arts sagacious dupes invent,
> To cheat themselves and gain the world's assent,
> The worst is—scripture warp'd from its intent.
>
> ("Progress of Error," 435-37)

Occasionally the third line will be an alexandrine, as in the following:

> Angelic gratulations rend the skies:
> Pride falls unpitied, never more to rise;
> Humility is crown'd; and faith receives the prize.
>
> ("Truth," 587-89)

These variations usually appear at structurally significant points, that is, to sum up a section or to conclude a poem. In a few instances Cowper uses a couplet with a second-line alexandrine for the same purpose:

> Till, tun'd at length to some immortal song,
> It sounds Jehovah's name, and pours his praise along.
>
> ("Conversation," 907-8)

More important is Cowper's metrical variation within lines: the caesura, for example, often varies from the first to the ninth syllable, a freedom frowned upon by Pope:

> Business or vain amusement, care or mirth,
> Divide the frail inhabitants of earth.
> Is duty a mere sport, or an employ?
> Life an intrusted talent, or a toy?
> Is there, as reason, conscience, scripture, say,
> Cause to provide for a great future day,
> When, earth's assign'd duration at an end,
> Man shall be summon'd and the dead attend?
> The trumpet—will it sound? the curtain rise?
> And show th' august tribunal of the skies,
> Where no prevarication shall avail,
> Where eloquence and artifice shall fail,
> The pride of arrogant distinctions fall,
> And conscience and our conduct judge us all?
>
> ("Retirement," 647-60)

In the various lines of this passage the caesura falls after the first, second, fourth, fifth, sixth, seventh, eighth, and ninth syllables, with the most extreme examples in the seventh and thirteenth lines. In addition there are relatively frequent metrical substitutions, mainly initial trochaic and internal pyrrhic feet; as well as the three-stress line 12 and variations between four- and five-stress lines elsewhere.

But Cowper's use of a non-epigrammatic norm provided the most important relaxing of the strict heroic couplet, in which his practice often resembles that of Churchill:

> Such knowledge, gain'd betimes, and which appears,
> Though solid, not too weighty for his years,
> Sweet in itself, and not forbidding sport,
> When health demands it, of athletic sort,
> Would make him—what some lovely boys have been,
> And more than one, perhaps, that I have seen—

> An evidence and reprehension both
> Of the mere school-boy's lean and tardy growth.
>
> ("Tirocinium," 650-57)

Although it is not freely enjambed, this passage does tend to weaken the individual couplet unity by a syntactic carry-over from the first line ("Such knowledge") to the fifth ("Would make him") to the completion of the main clause in the last couplet ("An evidence," etc.). Related to this non-epigrammatic norm is the prominence in Cowper's couplet poems of a nonparallel syntax, a structure that also tends to weaken the strict form of the heroic couplet and that anticipates the fully enjambed couplet of the early nineteenth century:

> Ingenious Art, with her expressive face,
> Steps forth to fashion and refine the race;
> Not only fills necessity's demand,
> But overcharges her capacious hand:
> Capricious taste itself can crave no more
> Than she supplies from her abounding store;
> She strikes out all that luxury can ask,
> And gains new vigour at her endless task.
>
> ("Charity," 97-104)

Here the thought proceeds by an accretion of details: Art "Steps forth," "fills," "overcharges," "supplies," "strikes out," and "gains new vigour"—all of which constitutes a forward-moving (rather than parallel) development.

Cowper's most interesting and successful use of couplets appears in his satire and nature descriptions. The satire lacks the facility and edge of a master, but it is sometimes nonetheless effective. Thus in "Conversation" he humorously if mildly chastises certain types of talkers:

> Vociferated logic kills me quite;
> A noisy man is always in the right—
> I twirl my thumbs, fall back into my chair,
> Fix on the wainscot a distressful stare,

And, when I hope his blunders are all out,
Reply discreetly—To be sure—no doubt! (113-18)

A graver coxcomb we may sometimes see,
Quite as absurd, though not so light as he:
A shallow brain behind a serious mask,
An oracle within an empty cask,
The solemn fop; significant and budge;
A fool with judges, amongst fools a judge;
He says but little, and that little said
Owes all its weight, like loaded dice, to lead.

(295-302)

And in "Retirement" the long portrait of the retired states-man, his initial enjoyment of country life, his subsequent boredom, and his final return to town, is a well-managed satiric study in contrasts. We are left with the following picture of him:

The prospect, such as might enchant despair,
He views it not, or sees no beauty there;
With aching heart, and discontented looks,
Returns at noon to billiards or to books,
But feels, while grasping at his faded joys,
A secret thirst of his renounc'd employs.
He chides the tardiness of ev'ry post,
Pants to be told of battles won or lost,
Blames his own indolence, observes, though late,
'Tis criminal to leave a sinking state,
Flies to the levee, and, receiv'd with grace,
Kneels, kisses hands, and shines again in place.

(469-80)

Earlier in the same passage occurs a picture of nature that may stand as typical of Cowper's well-modulated couplets used for description:

He knows indeed that, whether dress'd or rude,
Wild without art, or artfully subdu'd,
Nature in ev'ry form inspires delight,

But never mark'd her with so just a sight.
Her hedge-row shrubs, a variegated store,
With woodbine and wild roses mantled o'er,
Green balks and furrow'd lands, the stream that spreads
Its cooling vapour o'er the dewy meads,
Downs that almost escape th' inquiring eye,
That melt and fade into the distant sky,
Beauties he lately slighted as he pass'd,
Seem all created since he travell'd last.   (415-26)

Technically and structurally "Table Talk" provides the greatest unity in variety of any of Cowper's couplet poems as a whole. It is chiefly didactic satire, and is the only one of his couplet poems cast in the dramatic form of a dialogue. The subject matter divides the poem into three parts: (1) the virtues and vices of political leaders, particularly kings, (2) liberty versus tyranny, and (3) the poet's function with respect to these. Within this over-all structure smaller units are interestingly balanced and developed. Thus at the beginning appear two verse paragraphs which present contrasting pictures of good and bad leaders (lines 13-46) and in which the openings are syntactically parallel:

Let laurels, drench'd in pure Parnassian dews,
Reward his mem'ry, dear to ev'ry muse,
Who, with a courage of unshaken root,
In honour's field advancing his firm foot,
Plants it upon the line that justice draws,
And will prevail or perish in her cause . . .

But let eternal infamy pursue
The wretch to nought but his ambition true,
Who, for the sake of filling with one blast
The post-horns of all Europe, lays her waste . . .

The two passages are also approximately equal in length, the first containing sixteen and the second eighteen lines. Another remarkable syntactic parallel occurs in a later passage (lines 63-82), in which the first couplet:

> Oh! bright occasions of dispensing good,
> How seldom us'd, how little understood!

is followed by a series of eleven infinitive constructions, concluding with another repeated exclamation:

> Blest country, where these kingly glories shine;
> Blest England, if this happiness be thine!

As we have noted, this construction is especially characteristic of Churchill, whose influence upon Cowper is strongly marked in this poem.

The satire in "Table Talk" varies from light humorous attacks on pseudo-poets in the Horatian manner to heavier Juvenalian attempts to scourge a nation. In both kinds Cowper does nothing that had not been done better by Johnson and Churchill. Consider, for example, the attack on would-be poets:

> From him who rears a poem lank and long,
> To him who strains his all into a song;
> Perhaps some bonny Caledonian air,
> All birks and braes, though he was never there;
> Or, having whelp'd a prologue with great pains,
> Feels himself spent, and fumbles for his brains;
> A prologue interdash'd with many a stroke—
> An art contriv'd to advertise a joke,
> So that the jest is clearly to be seen,
> Not in the words—but in the gap between:
> Manner is all in all, whate'er is writ,
> The substitute for genius, sense, and wit.   (532-43)

There is satiric humor here, but it is somewhat forced; and the music and rhythms are wholly conventional. The heavier satire is no better managed, although its religious and moral overtones were no doubt more congenial to Cowper himself:

> Not only vice disposes and prepares
> The mind, that slumbers sweetly in her snares,
> To stoop to tyranny's usurp'd command,

And bend her polish'd neck beneath his hand
(A dire effect, by one of nature's laws
Unchangeably connected with its cause);
But Providence himself will intervene
To throw his dark displeasure o'er the scene.
All are his instruments; each form of war,
What burns at home, or threatens from afar,
Nature in arms, her elements at strife,
The storms that overset the joys of life,
Are but his rods to scourge a guilty land,
And waste it at the bidding of his hand.   (438-51)

In this passage most of the language and tone are conven-
tional, but the image of Providence throwing "his dark dis-
pleasure o'er the scene" stands out for its freshness and vigor.
Logically there is little need for the parenthesis in the third
couplet, and the opening figure of the mind (or is it vice?)
bending "her polish'd neck" is confused if not ridiculous.
Finally, some of Cowper's most typical couplets appear in his
portrait of Churchill, in which, at a time (1782) when that
great satirist's reputation was fast slipping, Cowper stoutly
defended his former friend:

If brighter beams than all he threw not forth,
'Twas negligence in him, not want of worth.
Surly and slovenly, and bold and coarse,
Too proud for art, and trusting in mere force,
Spendthrift alike of money and of wit,
Always at speed, and never drawing bit,
He struck the lyre in such a careless mood,
And so disdain'd the rules he understood,
The laurel seem'd to wait on his command;
He snatch'd it rudely from the muses' hand. (680-89)

Whatever else may be their virtues, the heroic-couplet
poems of Young and Cowper illustrate the persuasive power
of this poetic form. Throughout the eighteenth century such
was its influence that even poets not naturally inclined to do

so, became neo-classic satirists *malgré eux!* This kind of writing in this particular form was not their *forte;* but in order to secure public attention and success, both Young and Cowper turned first to couplets and satire. Only after these initial successes did each undertake to write his major work in blank verse: *Night Thoughts* and *The Task.*

Chapter VI

Goldsmith: The Didactic-Lyric

I

LIKE Dryden and Johnson, Oliver Goldsmith is a master both in poetry and in "the other harmony of prose." In poetry, again like Johnson, he is famous as the author of one poem, *The Deserted Village*, which is undoubtedly his best. But his use of the heroic couplet in a number of other poems, especially *The Traveller*, is distinctive enough to merit serious critical consideration. Also included in these are four of his six Epilogues, the short *Description of an Author's Bedchamber*, and the heroic couplets in his oratorio, *The Captive*, all of which reveal important characteristics of his handling of the form.

The *Description of an Author's Bedchamber* is interesting on several counts. As the first of Goldsmith's heroic-couplet poems to be printed, it shows his command of the traditional form. Technically the couplets are all end-stopped and extremely regular, with the great majority of the lines four- and five-stress and medially caesuraed after the fourth, fifth, or sixth syllable. The poem is logically divided into three parts. The first six lines locate the bedchamber with its inmate "stretch'd beneath a rug." The next twelve lines present a detailed description of the room; and the last couplet returns to the impoverished author:

> A nightcap deck'd his brows instead of bay,
> A cap by night—a stocking all the day.[1]

[1] All references to Goldsmith's poetry are to *The Poetical Works of Oliver Goldsmith* ed. Austin Dobson.

Goldsmith evidently thought highly of this poem, for he used most of its lines (with variations) again in *The Deserted Village* (lines 225-36). The couplet above, for example, later becomes:

> The chest contriv'd a double debt to pay,
> A bed by night, a chest of drawers by day.

And another couplet in the original version—

> The royal game of goose was there in view,
> And the twelve rules the royal martyr drew—

is later condensed into the single line: "The twelve good rules, the royal game of goose."

Of Goldsmith's epilogues, the one to *She Stoops to Conquer* is both clever and well constructed. Its ideas recapitulate the story of the drama with wit and satire. Structurally the epilogue has two parts: the introductory six lines and the main developments in the remaining twenty-nine. The second part is further subdivided into five sections, based upon a summary of the five acts of the play. The couplets are for the most part traditional, except for a pronounced use of feminine rhymes.

The epilogue written for a benefit performance for the actor Charles Lee Lewes is noteworthy for other reasons. It is highly dramatic, with effective use of dialogue and action. But more significant are certain technical characteristics of the couplets that create effects typical of Goldsmith's style at its best. A strong lyrical quality is one of these, created most importantly by the suppression of a normal stress in the third or fourth metrical foot of the line: for example,

> In thy black aspect every passion sleeps,
> The joy that dimples, and the woe that weeps.
> How hast thou fill'd the scene with all thy brood,
> Of fools pursuing, and of fools pursu'd!   (9-12)

Note the contrast in rhythm and tempo between the lines of

each couplet. The first and third lines are five-stress, with variations in the first foot. In the second and fourth lines, which are four-stress, the third foot is a pyrrhic of two unstressed syllables. The metrical substitution at this point gives the lines an anapestic lyrical swing, which is further enhanced by the meaning and music. Of the epilogue's forty-six lines, seventeen contain this third or fourth pyrrhic foot, a proportion that gives the entire poem a marked lyrical tone. Another device that reinforces the lyrical quality and is characteristic of Goldsmith's style is the frequent repetition of words with the effect of an echo. Of this the last line above is an example, as are the following:

> But for a head, yes, yes, I have a head.   (34)

> My horns! I'm told horns are the fashion now.   (36)

As individual poems two other epilogues are probably Goldsmith's best: the second of two that were unused but were "intended to have been spoken for *She Stoops to Conquer*" and the epilogue to *The Good Natur'd Man*. The one intended for *She Stoops to Conquer* presents a humorous application of an idea from Ariosto that the moon is the repository of things lost on earth. Goldsmith asks:

> But where's this place, this storehouse of the age?
> The Moon, says he:—but *I* affirm the Stage.
> At least in many things, I think, I see
> His lunar, and our mimic world agree.
>
> .   .   .   .   .   .
>
> Both prone to change, no settled limits fix,
> And sure the folks of both are lunatics.   (5-12)

This first part introduces a series of seven types of people who attend the theatre "to find their senses." The last part brings in the author, who ironically satirizes himself:

> Of all the tribe here wanting an adviser
> Our Author's the least likely to grow wiser.   (33-34)

Yes, he's far gone:—and yet some pity fix,
The English laws forbid to punish lunatics. (41-42)

The other striking characteristic of this epilogue is the large
proportion of feminine rhymes, which appear in eight of the
twenty-one couplets. The main effects of this variation are
a relaxing of the couplet form and a more lyrical, if less
forceful, movement, caused by the final extra syllable.

The epilogue to *The Good Natur'd Man* is in Gold-
smith's best manner. It is a light and humorous satire on
prologues and epilogues, suggesting that Goldsmith seriously
considered these appendages to drama to have outlived their
vogue and usefulness. The poem begins auspiciously:

> As puffing quacks some caitiff wretch procure
> To swear the pill, or drop, has wrought a cure;
> Thus on the stage, our play-wrights still depend
> For Epilogues and Prologues on some friend . . .

This passage plus the couplet that follows constitutes the first
of the three-part epilogue. The second and main part de-
scribes the author's amusing but unsuccessful attempts to find
"a rhyming friend to help him out." Of course they all
"Give him good words indeed, but no assistance." The
words take the form of lively witty dialogue, which Gold-
smith manages within couplets and even within lines as well
as Pope. One friend, for instance, refuses to help and sug-
gests someone else:

> "No, no; I've other contests to maintain;
> To-night I head our troops at Warwick Lane:
> Go, ask your manager." "Who, me? Your pardon;
> Those things are not our forte at Covent Garden."
>   (17-20)

In the last part the author puts himself at the mercy of the
audience, with the help, however, of a quotation from Shake-
speare and a paraphrase of Pope in the second and third lines:

Since then, unhelp'd, our bard must now conform
"To 'bide the pelting of this pitiless storm"—
Blame where you must, be candid where you can;
And be each critic the *Good Natur'd Man*.

Technically the couplets, all end-stopped, are relatively regular, the only exceptions being a few caesuras in extreme positions and the five pairs of feminine rhymes out of a total of seventeen couplets.

The heroic couplets in Goldsmith's oratorio, *The Captive*, have a special function, the nature of which tends to make them strictly traditional. They are the narrative thread of "recitatives" upon which the lyrical stanzas of the oratorio are strung. Throughout *The Captive* there are eighteen separate groups of couplets (totalling 142 lines), each one from four to twelve lines in length. As couplets they are largely regular: end-stopped, balanced, and medially caesuraed.

The history of Goldsmith's supposed translation of Vida's *Game of Chess*, a mock-heroic poem of 679 lines, is interesting as an object lesson in the relation between external and internal evidence of authorship. Since 1854 the poem has been generally accepted as Goldsmith's; but it is written in couplets technically so unlike all his other work that, on this ground alone, the critic would be justified in rejecting it as Goldsmith's. For one thing, there is a far greater proportion of triplets-with-alexandrines in this poem than anywhere else in Goldsmith—eighteen, in contrast, for example, to none in either *The Traveller* or *The Deserted Village*. The use of this device is so marked, in fact, that John Forster, the biographer who introduced *The Game of Chess* into the Goldsmith canon, felt impelled to explain it by the suggestion that in this solitary instance Goldsmith had reverted to "the manner of the great master of translation, Dryden."[2] In the second place, there is far more enjambment in *The Game*

[2] John Forster, *Oliver Goldsmith*, II, 236.

of Chess than in any other poem by Goldsmith, as the following typical example indicates:

> But tender Venus, with a pitying eye,
> Viewing the sad destruction that was nigh,
> Wink'd upon Phoebus (for the Goddess sat
> By chance directly opposite); at that
> Roused in an instant, young Apollo threw
> His eyes around the field his troops to view:
> Perceiv'd the danger, and with sudden fright
> Withdrew the Foot that he had sent to fight,
> And sav'd his trembling Queen by seasonable flight.
>
> (284-92)

The first and second couplets are partially run together because of their syntax: they are joined by the subject "Venus" in the one and its verb "Wink'd" in the other. Also in these couplets the two rhyme words "nigh" and "that" are unemphatic because in grammar and meaning they are relatively unimportant. The second and third couplets are fully enjambed, with a full stop within the line at the end of the parenthesis. The caesuras are not limited to medial positions, but vary from the fourth syllable to the eighth. And the passage concludes with a triplet-and-alexandrine, also an exception, as we have said, to Goldsmith's regular practice. Finally, as a full-fledged mock-heroic poem, *The Game of Chess* represents a kind of approach to the subject that Goldsmith, in his own work, shows no interest in whatsoever.

If the internal evidence for Goldsmith's authorship of *The Game of Chess* has always been extremely weak, if not nonexistent, what, we may ask, has happened to the external evidence that for so long as been accepted as proof? One authoritative answer appears in *The Cambridge Bibliography of English Literature*, for which Ronald S. Crane is the editor of the Goldsmith section. He lists the Vida translation among the "Spurious, Doubtful, and Lost Works" of the poet, and his comment on it follows:

The sole ground for the ascription was the belief that the manu-
script was in Goldsmith's hand. Since, however, it is now clear
that this belief was mistaken, and that the Game of Chess is
written in a hand that bears only the most superficial resemblance
to Goldsmith's, there can be no longer any reason for retaining
the poem in the canon.[3]

II

Although *The Deserted Village* is now generally accepted
as Goldsmith's best poem, Johnson considered *The Traveller*
the better of the two. Both poems, however, represent Gold-
smith at his best; and both reveal his mastery of the heroic
couplet. *The Traveller* is the more simply constructed: it
is a kind of panoramic poem, in which imaginatively (rather
than literally, as in *Cooper's Hill*) the poet "surveys" Italy,
Switzerland, France, and England. These four sections, with
an introduction and a conclusion, form the structure of the
poem. Other traditional characteristics, stemming mainly
from Pope, include the absence of triplets and alexandrines,
very little enjambment, a predominantly parallel syntax, and
emphatic masculine rhymes.

In *The Traveller* the parallel syntax often expresses
abrupt antitheses in thought, as in the following lines about
the Italian:

> Contrasted faults through all his manners reign;
> Though poor, luxurious; though submissive, vain;
> Though grave, yet trifling; zealous, yet untrue;
> And e'en in penance planning sins anew.   (127-30)

In larger units the balanced thought contrast takes such forms
as the following description of the Dutch natives:

> Thus, while around the wave-subjected soil
> Impels the native to repeated toil,
> Industrious habits in each bosom reign,

        [3] *The Cambridge Bibliography of English Literature,* ed. F. E. Bateson, II,
646.

And industry begets a love of gain.
Hence all the good from opulence that springs,
With all those ills superfluous treasure brings,
Are here displayed. Their much-lov'd wealth imparts
Convenience, plenty, elegance, and arts;
But view them closer, craft and fraud appear,
E'en liberty itself is barter'd here.
At gold's superior charms all freedom flies,
The needy sell it, and the rich man buys;
A land of tyrants, and a den of slaves,
Here wretches seek dishonourable graves,
And calmly bent, to servitude conform,
Dull as their lakes that slumber in the storm. (297-312)

The passage is divided exactly at the middle: the first eight
lines picture an attractive virtuous people, the second eight
their sharply contrasting vices. And within couplets and
even within lines the balanced syntax with thought antithesis
continues, becoming most apparent in such lines as "The
needy sell it, and the rich man buys; A land of tyrants, and
a den of slaves," etc.

Another form of parallelism (also characteristic, as we
have seen, of Churchill and Johnson) is the repetition of
identical syntactic structures. Note, for instance, the three-
fold "whatever" construction in the following passage:

Whatever fruits in different climes were found,
That proudly rise, or humbly court the ground;
Whatever blooms in torrid tracts appear,
Whose bright succession decks the varied year;
Whatever sweets salute the northern sky
With vernal lives that blossom but to die . . . (113-18)

In these ways and in others (such as the predominance of
the four- and five-stress line and the medial caesura) Gold-
smith carries on the neo-classic tradition.

In other ways, however, his own contribution to the tra-
dition is marked. One of these is the notable way in which

he uses word repetition for a variety of effects. The simplest
function of this device is for emphasis, as in the following
couplets (I have italicized the key words):

> Heavens! *how unlike* their Belgic sires of old!
> Rough, poor, content, ungovernably bold;
> War in each breast, and freedom on each brow;
> *How much unlike* the sons of Britain now!   (313-16)

In addition to emphasis there is thought progression in this
repetition, for in the first couplet the Dutch are simply "un-
like" their own ancestors, while in the second they are "much
unlike" the English. A more intricate and important use of
repetition gives not only emphasis but increased structural
unity by knitting the couplets together. Thus in the follow-
ing passage "the peasant's hut" and "his humble shed" at the
beginning and end of the two couplets and the once-repeated
"sees" in the middle function in this manner:

> Though poor the peasant's hut, his feasts though small,
> He sees his little lot the lot of all;
> Sees no contiguous palace rear its head
> To shame the meanness of his humble shed ... (177-80)

Finally, this device in its greatest complexity yields effects
that are most characteristic of Goldsmith and that therefore
merit analysis:

> Lakes, forests, cities, plains, extending wide,
> The pomp of kings, the shepherd's humbler pride.
> When thus Creation's charms around combine,
> Amidst the store, should thankless pride repine?
> Say, should the philosophic mind disdain
> That good, which makes each humbler bosom vain?
> Let school-taught pride dissemble all it can,
> These little things are great to little man;
> And wiser he, whose sympathetic mind
> Exults in all the good of all mankind.   (35-44)

The general theme arises out of the implied contrast between

"The pomp of kings" and "the shepherd's humbler pride."
The contrast turns on two kinds of pride: that of kings and
that of the "little man." All that follows is a variation on
the thought of the first couplet, which concludes the pre-
ceding verse paragraph and is thus closely united to the suc-
ceeding one. The idea of pride in its two aspects dominates
the entire passage; for "thankless pride" and "school-taught
pride" are allied to "The pomp of kings," whereas the "hum-
bler pride" in "each humbler bosom" understands that
"These little things are great to little man." This elaborate
contrast is finally resolved in the last couplet, where both the
pride of kings and that of shepherds are seen as complemen-
tary parts of a unified whole—"all the good of all mankind."

From another point of view, this characteristic of word
repetition greatly strengthens the lyrical quality of Gold-
smith's couplets. The reason for this is, of course, a matter
of music—the echoing of repeated sound combinations, es-
pecially if the repetition is only partial. Oliver Elton has
remarked the lyrical beauties of the second verse paragraph
of *The Traveller* (lines 11-22), with its variations upon the
word "blessings."[4] In another less familiar passage there
are impressive plays upon the words "Thine," "Freedom,"
and "blessings":

> Thine, Freedom, thine the blessings pictur'd here,
> Thine are those charms that dazzle and endear;
> Too bless'd indeed, were such without alloy,
> But foster'd e'en by Freedom, ills annoy . . .   (335-38)

In terms of music, alliteration is of course another kind
of repetition of sounds. Although alliteration is marked in
all heroic-couplet poetry, Goldsmith's use of it for purely
lyrical effects is especially noteworthy. Sometimes it subtly
functions to tie couplets together, as in the following:

> The naked negro, panting at the line,
> Boasts of his golden sands and palmy wine,

[4] *Op. cit.,* I, 105-6.

> Basks in the glare, or stems the tepid wave,
> And thanks his gods for all the good they gave. (69-72)

Between the two couplets there is what may be called vertical alliteration, for in the second and third lines the *b*, *g*, *s*, and *w* sounds appear in identical positions in both lines ("Boasts" and "Basks," "golden" and "glare," "sands" and "stems," "wine" and "wave"). In other places alliteration combines with word repetition and variation in tempo to achieve striking lyrical effects:

> There all around the gentlest breezes stray,
> There gentle music melts on ev'ry spray;
> Creation's mildest charms are there combin'd,
> Extremes are only in the master's mind! (321-24)

The repetition of "There" and "gentle" and the dominant alliterative *m* sounds combine with the thought to create a lyrical mood, which is further enhanced by the lilting movement of the last line with its pyrrhic third metrical foot.

Most of the traditional neo-classic uses of music and movement may of course be found in *The Traveller*. There is the frequent emphasis upon alliteration within the line: "Allures from far, yet, as I follow, flies" (28). A more familiar passage illustrates both effective alliteration and the sharp change in tempo which the masters of the couplet exploited, from Dryden on:

> Stern o'er each bosom reason holds her state,
> With daring aims irregularly great;
> Pride in their port, defiance in their eye,
> I see the lords of human kind pass by,
> Intent on high designs, a thoughtful band,
> By forms unfashion'd, fresh from Nature's hand;
> Fierce in their native hardiness of soul,
> True to imagin'd right, above control,
> While e'en the peasant boasts these rights to scan,
> And learns to venerate himself as man. (325-34)

The third line is impressively alliterative in the traditional way. In line six, however, the emphatic *f* sounds function also to relate that couplet to its successor, which opens with the strongly accented word "Fierce." Also in the first couplet of this passage, note the change of pace between the lines: the first is slow-moving, with stopped consonants and long vowels dominant and with five full stresses; the second, on the other hand, is light and speedy, a four-stress line varied by the polysyllabic word "irregularly." The same contrast in tempo, for similar reasons, exists between the lines of the last couplet.

The general idea of *The Traveller*, as is well known, owes much to Goldsmith's great friend, Samuel Johnson, which may in part account for Johnson's preference for it. Its broad theme is "the vanity of human wishes," a subject that Johnson was more competent than Goldsmith to deal with. The lines,

> Vain, very vain, my weary search to find
> That bliss which only centres in the mind,

need only be compared with the concluding couplet of Johnson's poem:

> With these celestial wisdom calms the mind,
> And makes the happiness she does not find.

Even the rhymes, although in reverse order, are the same; and, we remember, Johnson is supposed to have written eight of the last ten lines of *The Traveller* himself.

The peculiar flavor and essence of Goldsmith's heroic couplet appear most often and most brilliantly in *The Deserted Village*. In this instance it was sound critical judgment, supported by the steady approval of generations of readers, that has included this poem in all the anthologies of the period. In general appeal, also critically defensible, *The Deserted Village* has only one competitor in the eighteenth century: Gray's *Elegy*. The reasons for this remarkable appeal are partly matters of ideology and personality, with which the present study is not concerned. But there are also many structural and technical considerations (more critical than historical) that bear importantly on the subject.

In total structure *The Deserted Village* is less obviously and mechanically put together than *The Traveller;* and, although both are philosophic-descriptive poems, *The Deserted Village* is not panoramic. Instead of surveying any kind of prospect, literally or imaginatively, the poet introduces contrasting themes that reappear with variations throughout the poem. The ideas expressed in these themes are commonplaces of eighteenth-century thought. "Ill fares the land, to hast'ning ills a prey, Where wealth accumulates, and men decay" is a continuation of the Shaftesburian side of the Shaftesbury–Mandeville controversy about the social effects of luxury. This controversy held a peculiar fascination for the poets of the time, especially for Pope, Thomson, Akenside, the Wartons, Goldsmith, and Burns, all of whom took the same side. Goldsmith's poem is therefore not significant for the power or originality of its thought. What makes it a great poem is his use of the heroic couplet to create a masterful symphony of moods. As a corollary to this achievement, the couplet becomes more frequently and consistently lyrical in *The Deserted Village* than in any other neo-classic poem.

Goldsmith's well-known interest in music (he is said to have described his Continental wanderings as "fluting and disputing" his way through Europe!) suggests an approach to his poem that is fully substantiated by the nature of the poem itself. In structure and mood *The Deserted Village* may be likened to the sonata form, the three parts of which present the exposition, development, and recapitulation of two major themes. Part I (lines 1-56) gives an exposition of the moods of joy and sorrow, based upon a descriptive-

philosophic treatment of past rural happiness in England
and present rural desolation. The thought relationship be-
tween the two moods is summarized in the famous lines:

> Ill fares the land, to hast'ning ills a prey,
> Where wealth accumulates, and men decay:
> Princes and lords may flourish, or may fade;
> A breath can make them, as a breath has made;
> But a bold peasantry, their country's pride,
> When once destroy'd, can never be supplied. (51-56)

The lyrical quality of this passage is everywhere admitted.
It arises, of course, from the complex interrelationship of
meaning, music, and rhythm, in which we may see Gold-
smith's poetic art at its best. The first line, for instance, con-
tains word repetition with the effect of an echo; but it is not
mere repetition, for the first "ill" is an adverb and the second
a plural noun. The fourth line is also noteworthy in this
respect, with its repetition of "breath" and partial repetition
of "make" and "made." The movement of the first two
lines is sharply contrasted, the first being a stately six-stress
line and the second a quick four-stress one, in which the
polysyllabic "accumulates" increases the tempo. Five of the
six lines contain a substituted pyrrhic third or fourth metrical
foot, which suggests a moving anapestic rhythm. This fact
also accounts for the suppression of one normal stress in all
of these lines.

Part II of *The Deserted Village* is its main section (lines
57-394)—the development of the two themes introduced in
Part I, the moods of joy and sorrow. The first unit of this
thematic development (lines 57-112) presents a brief alter-
nation between the two moods, signalized by the introductory
clauses: "A time there was" and "But times are alter'd."
This alternation of the themes is followed by a longer pas-
sage (lines 82-112) that prepares for the first major develop-
ment and that in itself communicates an intermingled mood

of joy-in-sadness. It describes the poet's hopes for a happy
retirement to his native village of Auburn, hopes that, in the
light of the present rural desolation, are doomed to dis-
appointment:

> I still had hopes, my long vexations pass'd,
> Here to return—and die at home at last.
> O blest retirement, friend to life's decline,
> Retreats from care, that never must be mine . . .
>
> (95-98)

The second unit of the development (lines 113-236)
elaborates the mood of joy by a poetic recreation of the vil-
lage's past. This unit is subdivided into the four famous
passages: the picture of the general happiness of the village,
the portrait of the village preacher, the portrait of the village
schoolmaster, and the picture of the village tavern where
the natives met. In all of these descriptions Goldsmith's
sentiment, humor, and genius for the right word appear, as,
for example:

> In arguing too, the parson own'd his skill,
> For e'en through vanquish'd, he could argue still;
> While words of learned length and thund'ring sound
> Amazed the gazing rustics rang'd around,
> And still they gaz'd, and still the wonder grew,
> That one small head could carry all he knew. (211-16)

This is sharp, objective, Chaucerian portraiture, with its
subtle combinations of wit and satire ("For e'en though van-
quish'd, he could argue still"), the Goldsmith echo ("In
arguing too . . . he could argue still," "Amazed the gazing
rustics . . . And still they gaz'd, and still . . . "), and the
Goldsmith music and movement.

The third unit of Part II (lines 237-394) elaborates in a
similar way the contrasting mood of sorrow by emphasizing
the present desolate condition of the Auburn countryside and
the natives who have had to leave it. Here also there are

four subdivisions: (1) a general picture of the present ruin
of the countryside, stressing the evils of luxury versus the
virtues of poverty (237-302); (2) the present condition of
the poor natives, including the horrors of their going to the
city (303-36); (3) the greater horrors of their going abroad
to the colonies (337-62); and (4) the pathetic picture of their
enforced home-leaving, concluding with a diatribe against
luxury, the cause of their suffering (363-94). The central
thought and emotion of the entire unit are concentrated in
the following passage, with its dramatic, almost "metaphysi-
cal," concluding line:

> Thus fares the land, by luxury betray'd;
> In nature's simplest charms at first array'd;
> But verging to decline, its splendours rise,
> Its vistas strike, its palaces surprise;
> While scourg'd by famine from the smiling land,
> The mournful peasant leads his humble band;
> And while he sinks, without one arm to save,
> The country blooms—a garden, and a grave. (295-302)

The last thirty-six lines, which form Part III of *The
Deserted Village*, represent a kind of recapitulation of the
themes previously developed. This part begins with a re-
statement of the mood of sorrow:

> E'en now the devastation is begun,
> And half the business of destruction done;
> E'en now, methinks, as pond'ring here I stand,
> I see the rural virtues leave the land . . .   (395-98)

The rural virtues are then dramatically personified as they
leave the land: "contented toil," "hospitable care," "piety,"
"steady loyalty and faithful love." After which "sweet
Poetry" is introduced, and the remaining lines form an
apostrophe that relieves the sadness by a revival of hope:

> Still let thy voice, prevailing over time,
> Redress the rigours of th' inclement clime;

> Aid slighted truth; with thy persuasive strain
> Teach erring man to spurn the rage of gain;
> Teach him, that states of native strength possess'd,
> Though very poor, may still be very bless'd . . . (421-26)

It is thus in its totality, as well as in verse paragraphs, couplets, and individual lines, that *The Deserted Village* may be described critically as a didactic-lyric poem.

All the qualities of the heroic couplet characteristic of Goldsmith, lyric and otherwise, appear at their maturest in this poem. The following passage reveals some of them, including one that does not often appear elsewhere:

> Yet count our gains. This wealth is but a name
> That leaves our useful products still the same.
> Not so the loss. The man of wealth and pride
> Takes up a space that many poor supplied;
> Space for his lake, his park's extended bounds,
> Space for his horses, equipage, and hounds . . . (273-78)

The full stops within lines 1 and 3 ("Yet count our gains. . . . Not so the loss") are typical of the enjambed couplet, yet all of these are rigidly end-stopped; so Goldsmith secures certain effects of the one without sacrificing those of the other. Another effect of this device is the reëmphasis upon the parallel structure, which is further complicated by the thought contrast between "gains" and "loss." And the device also unifies the first two couplets by syntactic repetition. In terms of movement, these short constructions give a staccato-like effect to the whole passage, an effect that is greatly enhanced by the monosyllabic vocabulary. The other notable characteristic is the familiar word repetition ("space"), which not only ties together the second and third couplets, but also contributes its share of lyric echo.

Verbal music is of course pronounced throughout the poem, with traditional alliteration and assonance present in a marked degree. Occasionally "vertical" alliteration is used to unify two couplets, as in the following instance:

As some fair female unadorn'd and plain,
Secure to please while youth confirms her reign,
Slights every borrow'd charm that dress supplies,
Nor shares with art the triumph of her eyes ... (287-90)

where the *s* sounds (especially in "Secure" and "Slights")
perform this function.   More often, however, the vowel and
consonant music is combined with word repetition to create an
intricate pattern of harmonies:

These were thy charms, sweet village; sports like these,
With sweet succession, taught e'en toil to please;
These round thy bowers their cheerful influence shed,
These were thy charms—But all these charms are fled.
Sweet smiling village, loveliest of the lawn,
Thy sports are fled, and all thy charms withdrawn. (31-36)

Here too the *s* sounds predominate, with the consonants *t*
and *l* as runners-up; but this alliteration is strikingly re-
inforced and qualified by the five-fold repetition of "these"
and the four-fold repetition of "charms," both of which are
melodic combinations of sounds.   And supporting this word
music is the firm parallel syntax of the passage, to which the
word repetition also contributes.   Finally, note the more
complex repetition of whole clauses, sometimes identically
and sometimes with variations, in the first, fourth, and sixth
lines: "These were thy charms . . . These were thy charms
. . . all these charms are fled . . . Thy sports are fled."   For
that matter, even "sweet village" and "Sweet smiling village"
might well be described as incremental repetition of a special
kind.

It is thus in the realm of tone and movement that Gold-
smith contributes most memorably to the heroic couplet.   The
new music which he injects into the old form has often been
remarked.   This emphasis upon music, as Goldsmith uses it,
is attended by dangers as well as advantages.   When his
thought is trivial, the music further dilutes it into weak sen-

timentality; but where the ideas are themselves strong and noble (as in the famous "Ill fares the land" passage), the music and the rhythms create a profound and unique interpretation of the experience. In such instances, the couplets, which are in the best sense didactic, are expanded by the music into lyric territory, without losing their moral and rhetorical grandeur of statement. Johnson and Goldsmith are the masters of these effects in neo-classic poetry. The result in Johnson is that "pathos in isolation" which we have already noted. In Goldsmith, where these effects are more pervasive, there is often pathos, but it is more social than individual and hence it misses the near-tragic personal isolation of *The Vanity of Human Wishes*.

Chapter VII

Crabbe: Neo-Classic Narrative

I

THE reputation of George Crabbe today owes most of its lingering vitality to one poem. In his standard anthology piece, *The Village*, he is usually accorded the faint praise of having written, in traditional couplets, a grim and realistic rejoinder to Goldsmith. As for Crabbe's later work, it "may be looked upon as little more than an expansion" of *The Village*. The adequacy of this assertion by the editors of the Oxford edition of Crabbe we can at least test; and in so doing we shall be dealing with a poet who was, in a very real sense, the last of the Augustans. It is common knowledge that Crabbe wrote wholly in the neo-classic tradition, but that he added anything to the tradition perhaps requires demonstration. What he added was a masterful adaptation of the heroic couplet to narrative. This achievement not only places Crabbe among the great storytellers in verse— it also reveals the vitality of the heroic couplet almost two hundred years after Waller's earliest use of it in 1623.

In Crabbe's earlier and better known poems there are numerous anticipations of his later major work; but none of these completely fulfills the formula for the "tale" as he developed it. In *The Village*, for example, appear the creation of atmosphere through description and the creation of character by means of the type portrait. Thus described is the village's depressing background:

> There thistles stretch their prickly arms afar,
> And to the ragged infant threaten war;
> There poppies, nodding, mock the hope of toil;
> There the blue bugloss points the sterile soil;
> Hardy and high, above the slender sheaf,
> The slimy mallow waves her silky leaf;
> O'er the young shoot the charlock throws a shade,
> And clasping tares cling round the sickly blade;
> With mingled tints the rocky coasts abound,
> And a sad splendour vainly shines around.[1]

Here the modifiers, of which Crabbe was always in danger of
using too many, add effectively to the total picture: "ragged
infant," "sterile soil," "slimy mallow," "sickly blade," "sad
splendour," "vainly shines," etc.

As portraiture, we may consider the following lines about
an old man:

> Oft may you see him, when he tends the sheep,
> His winter-charge, beneath the hillock weep;
> Oft hear him murmur to the winds that blow
> O'er his white locks and bury them in snow,
> When, roused by rage and muttering in the morn,
> He mends the broken hedge with icy thorn:—
>   "Why do I live, when I desire to be
> "At once from life and life's long labour free?"
>
>   (I, 200-7)

And his soliloquy continues for eighteen more lines. In this
passage and throughout the whole portrait (I, 179-225), the
details create a typical old man who is a model of virtue un-
rewarded because he is poor. Furthermore, the device of
having the old man speak foreshadows the action through
dialogue in the later tales.

In *The Parish Register* we approach more closely to the
full-fledged tale. This poem is a kind of "Spoon-River

---

[1] Book I, lines 69-78: unless otherwise indicated, all references to Crabbe's
work are from *George Crabbe, Poems*, ed. A. W. Ward.

Anthology," consisting of a series of portraits drawn from the lower levels of rural life. Through the device of describing the births, marriages, and deaths of the past year, the poet in the person of the village rector proceeds from the baptism of the illegitimate child of Lucy, the proud miller's daughter, at the beginning to the burial of old Ralph Dibble at the end.

Some of the portraits are that and nothing more, but many of them go beyond the status of a static picture and become sketches of the life and fortunes of a particular character. The account of Phoebe Dawson is one of these. It tells the kind of story usually associated with Crabbe—the story of a beautiful innocent country girl, who is too weak to resist temptation. She falls and is forsaken by her lover soon after they are married. The account of Lucy Collins is another sketch of the same kind, although it is told with more concentration and economy. Indeed the end is foreshadowed in the opening couplet:

> For Lucy Collins happier days had been,
> Had Footman Daniel scorn'd his native green.
>
> (II, 313-14)

Both sketches are straightforward narrative that makes no use of dialogue.

But not all the sketches in *The Parish Register* are sordid and tragic. A few of them are light and humorously satiric, anticipating similar kinds of tales later. Thus when a foundling is left in the parish, the "village sires" solemnly meet to give it a name, a difficult problem,

> For he who lent it to a babe unknown,
> Censorious men might take it for his own:
> They look'd about, they gravely spoke to all,
> And not one Richard answer'd to the call.
> Next they inquired the day, when, passing by,
> Th' unlucky peasant heard the stranger's cry:

> This known, how food and raiment they might give,
> Was next debated—for the rogue would live;
> At last, with all their words and work content,
> Back to their homes the prudent vestry went,
> And Richard Monday to the workhouse sent.
>
> (I, 700-10)

In the end Richard Monday, neglected and mistreated in the poorhouse, makes his way in the world so successfully that he dies rich—

> But, to his native place severely just,
> He left a pittance bound in rigid trust,   (I, 761-62)

that is both an embarrassment and humiliation to the parish.

Finally, the experiment with dialogue begins in some of the sketches. In one, Roger Cuff, who has been forty years at sea, returns disguised to test the hospitality of his nephews and niece:

> Then the gay Niece the seeming pauper press'd:—
> "Turn, Nancy, turn, and view this form distress'd;
> "Akin to thine is this declining frame,
> "And this poor beggar claims an Uncle's name."
> "Avaunt! begone!" the courteous maiden said,
> "Thou vile impostor! Uncle Roger's dead:
> "I hate thee, beast; thy look my spirit shocks;
> "Oh! that I saw thee starving in the stocks!"
> "My gentle niece!" he said—and sought the wood.
>
> (III, 771-79)

This is somewhat flamboyant, but the author's restrained irony (in "the *courteous* maiden said" and "My *gentle* niece!"—italics mine) counterbalances the rhetorical excesses of the dialogue.

In *The Borough* Crabbe moves still closer to the tale as he finally developed it. In this series of twenty-four "letters" his materials are "the sea, and the country in the immediate vicinity; the dwellings, and the inhabitants; some incidents and characters, with an exhibition of morals and manners. . . ."[2] In his treatment of them, Crabbe makes the incidents and characters stand out more independently; they are structurally more complete in themselves; and technically the couplets become more flexible and generally appropriate for narration and dialogue. It is noteworthy too that the sketches become progressively better and that the account of "Peter Grimes" in Letter XXII is probably the best of them all.

Although it lacks the subtlety and finish of the later tales at their best, "Peter Grimes" contains most of the ingredients of the typical Crabbe story. Structurally it is divided into three parts. The first fifty-eight lines are introductory exposition, giving the antecedents and character of Peter Grimes. The next 106 lines vividly recount his cruelty in the murder of three apprentices. The last 110 lines deal with the social and psychological reactions to these crimes, culminating in Grimes's hallucinations and death.

Foreshadowing to create suspense appears early in the story, where, for example, young Peter turns savagely on his father,

> And while old Peter in amazement stood,
> Gave the hot spirit to his boiling blood;—
> How he, with oath and furious speech, began
> To prove his freedom and assert the man;
> And when the parent check'd his impious rage,
> How he had cursed the tyranny of age . . . (20-25)

And later we are told about Peter that "no success could please his cruel soul, He wish'd for one to trouble and control" (53-54). Suspense is maintained in other ways, one of which makes use of grim humorous understatement. At one point, just before the first apprentice dies, Peter is beating him—

---

[2] *Crabbe*, ed. Ward, I, 268.

> . . . and some, on hearing cries,
> Said calmly, "Grimes is at his exercise."   (77-78)

The creation of atmosphere adds greatly to the total effect of the story, especially the kind that is a favorite with Crabbe. He often describes the natural background of human actions in such a way that nature powerfully reflects the human situation. Thus when the reaction to Grimes's cruelty sets in, he is ostracized by society and begins to suffer from his own conscience, all of which is implied symbolically in nature itself:

> When tides were neap, and, in the sultry day,
> Through the tall bounding mud-banks made their way,
> Which on each side rose swelling, and below
> The dark warm flood ran silently and slow:
> There anchoring, Peter chose from man to hide,
> There hang his head, and view the lazy tide
> In its hot slimy channel slowly glide;
>
> .   .   .   .   .   .
>
> He nursed the feelings these dull scenes produce,
> And loved to stop beside the opening sluice;
> Where the small stream, confined in narrow bound,
> Ran with a dull, unvaried, sadd'ning sound;
> Where all presented to the eye or ear
> Oppress'd the soul with misery, grief, and fear. (181-204)

A great deal of dialogue appears in this story, particularly in the third part where it reinforces the dramatic situation of Grimes's hallucinations. The dialogue in couplets tends, however, to be rather stiff and mechanical, although there are exceptions, as in Grimes's account of the three ghosts that plague him:

> "To hear and mark them daily was my doom,
> "And 'Come,' they said, with weak, sad voices, 'come.'
> "To row away with all my strength I try'd;
> "But there were they, hard by me in the tide,

"The three unbodied forms—and 'Come,' still 'come,'
                                    they cried."

                                                    (323-27)

Technically the couplets are not exceptional; they are for the most part traditional and, like the dialogue, are too often stiff and mechanical.

II

Although "Peter Grimes" is well constructed and contains some powerful scenes, it is on the whole too sensational and melodramatic to rank among Crabbe's best stories. Compared to them, it is like a Gothic novel in relationship to one by Fielding or Thackeray. It does, however, point the way to Crabbe's full poetic achievement in narrative, which first appeared two years later—in the *Tales* (1812)—and was continued in his last work, *Tales of the Hall* (1819).

In these poems Crabbe's use of the heroic couplet for narrative is the most interesting and successful of any since Dryden. In Crabbe's hands, however, the couplet itself does not attain that mastery of form that it does in the work of Churchill, Johnson, and Pope. Like Goldsmith's and Cowper's, Crabbe's couplet is more relaxed. The most obvious sign of this relaxing is his regular use of the triplet and alexandrine, a practice that he shares with Dryden. These exceptions to the couplet form Crabbe employs for definite purposes: to secure variety, emphasis, and structural demarcation in the development of the story. Thus in "The Mother" (*Tales*, No. VIII), thirty of the poem's 360 lines are grouped into ten triplets, of which nine have a hexameter and one a pentameter third line. The triplets are spaced evenly throughout the poem, and six are used simply as variations. The remaining four mark points of emphasis and structural change—uses that are similar to one function of the couplet in Elizabethan drama, that of pointing up and concluding blank verse scenes.[3]

[3] Specifically Crabbe's four triplets function as follows: (1) to sum up and conclude the introductory section of the story (lines 62-65), (2) to point up the

Crabbe's adaptation of the couplet form to short narrative
is in itself a brilliant achievement.   As he uses it, the end-
stopped couplet adds point and concentration to the narra-
tive.   In "The Mother" note, for example, how the couplets
give a tone of sharp finality to the following ideas:

> Hope, ease, delight, the thoughts of dying gave,
> Till Lucy spoke with fondness of the grave;
> She smiled with wasted form, but spirit firm,
> And said, she left but little for the worm.   (294-97)

This passage also contains a grimly humorous shock that is
in a sense "metaphysical"—an effect that the couplets con-
tribute to and that F. R. Leavis would call the operation of a
kind of "wit."[4]   The touch of this wit, pointed up by the
couplet form and often making excellent use of dialogue, ap-
pears throughout the *Tales*.   Another instance occurs in the
story of "Jesse and Colin" (No. XIII), a pair of lovers who,
after much difficulty, are brought together:

> The youth embolden'd, yet abash'd, now told
> His fondest wish, nor found the maiden cold;
> The mother smiling whisper'd—"Let him go
> "And seek the license!" Jesse answer'd, "No":
> But Colin went . . .   (513-17)

And we find, as often happens in Crabbe, that the maiden's
"no" means "yes."

Although Crabbe's mature style is not epigrammatic, he
could write in this manner, both seriously and humorously;
and when he does so, the effect is a heightening of summary
and emphasis in the narrative.   Thus in "Arabella" (*Tales*,
No. IX) the beautiful bluestocking heroine is applauded by

---

next section about the vain mother and her elder daughter's beauty (83-86); (3)
to summarize the character of Lucy, the younger daughter, and foreshadow the
tragedy of her life (112-15); and (4) to emphasize the uncertainty of the lovers'
status and maintain suspense about the outcome (161-64).

[4] *Op. cit.*, pp. 124-29.

the mothers of the town as a model for their daughters; Crabbe comments on the results:

> From such applause disdain and anger rise,
> And envy lives where emulation dies.   (17-18)

The same Arabella is subtly ridiculed after she "becomes the wonder of the town":

> And strangers, coming, all were taught t' admire
> The learned lady, and the lofty spire.   (35-36)

From *Tales of the Hall* consider the ironic question put by the disillusioned lover ("The Elder Brother") to his faithless Rosabella:

> " 'My faith must childish in your sight appear,
> " 'Who have been faithful—to how many, dear?' "
> (585-86)

Or, in "The Maid's Story," the old maid's concise summary of a supposed frailty among women:

> "Secrets with girls, like loaded guns with boys,
> "Are never valued till they make a noise."   (84-85)

And, finally, the Old Bachelor's epigrammatic expression of the inappropriateness of loving a young girl at his age— "When it was almost treason to be kind" (145).

Special syntactic constructions characteristic of the heroic couplet also add their special effects to Crabbe's handling of narrative. Among these, as we noted in the work of earlier poets, are the uses of word order which give balance and antithesis, as well as unexpected variations of them. The simplest is of course the balanced line of two similarly constructed elements, separated by a preposition or a conjunction:

> The scatter'd hovels on the barren green.
> ("The Lover's Journey," 350)

> He reached the mansion, and he saw the maid.
> ("The Lover's Journey," 327)

To cause some wonder or excite some fear.

                          ("The Dumb Orators," 121)

Such lines usually contain four stresses, with the middle accent suppressed.

In the balanced construction expectation is always rewarded. Just as often, however, Crabbe introduces elements that are out of balance or makes the balance one between unequal parts; the result is an unexpected structural development:

Yet few there were who needed less the art
To hide an error, or a grace impart.

                          ("Lady Barbara," 267-68)

In the first half of the second line the normal word order ("to hide an error") leads us to expect the same order in the second half; instead we are surprised by the inversion: "or a grace impart." Similarly in the line,

She saw the wonders, she the mercies felt,

                          ("The Mother," 307)

the verb-object inversion in the second half creates an imbalance within the otherwise perfectly balanced line. When the two parts are unequal, the element that makes them so becomes conspicuous. Thus in the line,

He rich and proud—I very proud and poor,

                          ("The Hall," 296)

the balanced elements are "He rich and proud—I . . . proud and poor"; the adverb "very" therefore provides the inequality and attracts our attention. There is also the contrast in meaning between rich and poor at the beginning and end of the line. In the following line,

"She will be kind, and I again be blest,"

                          ("The Lover's Journey," 325)

the word "again" makes the balance unequal. Finally, there

is the kind of partial balance that involves the repetition of words as well as special uses of word order:

> There went the nymph, and made her strong complaints,
> Painting her woe as injured feeling paints.
>
> ("The Widow's Tale," 96-97)

> Now weak, now lively, changing with the day,
> These were his feelings, and he felt his way.
>
> ("The Convert," 91-92)

Sometimes whole passages will be united by balance and contrast, as in the following lines about two types of women:

> Those are like wax—apply them to the fire,
> Melting, they take th' impression you desire;
> Easy to mould, and fashion as you please,
> And again moulded with an equal ease;
> Like melted iron these the forms retain,
> But once impress'd will never melt again.
>
> ("Resentment," 11-16)

The two types are introduced by balanced elements—"Those are like wax . . . Like melted iron these"; but within them the word order is reversed, and "those" contrasts with "these." In addition to rhyme, the lines of the second couplet are held together by the partial repetition of "Easy to mould" and "Again moulded"; and the whole passage is united by the repetition of the ideas of melting and taking an impression. All of these qualities appear in single lines, couplets, and groups of couplets; but for narrative they are most significant when they control a whole verse paragraph, as in the following from "The Frank Courtship" (*Tales*, No. VI):

> Peace in the sober house of Jonas dwelt,
> Where each his duty and his station felt:
> Yet not that peace some favour'd mortals find,
> In equal views and harmony of mind;

Not the soft peace that blesses those who love,
Where all with one consent in union move;
But it was that which one superior will
Commands, by making all inferiors still;
Who bids all murmurs, all objections cease,
And with imperious voice announces—Peace!

(23-32)

In these ten lines the most obvious unifying device is the
repetition of the word "peace": it not only encloses the pas-
sage at the beginning and end, but holds everything together
by reappearing in the third and fifth lines as well. In terms
of thought and syntax, the paragraph is also effectively and
characteristically unified. The first couplet, ending with a
colon, asserts the peace that reigns in the house. The next
two couplets, introduced by "yet not," define the kind of
peace by contrasts; and the last two couplets, beginning with
"but," complete the definition by a positive description.
Structurally, therefore, the passage is divided into three
parts: the first couplet, the next two, and the last two; and
in thought and syntax the conclusion takes us back to the
beginning.

This passage appears early in the introduction of "The
Frank Courtship," where its function is to characterize the
home atmosphere in which the heroine grew up. The pre-
cise structure, the syntactic balance and repetition, parallel
and reinforce the qualities of precision, order, and control
which the father, Jonas, imposes on his wife and daughter.
In an impressive way, therefore, not only the sound but also
the syntax is made to echo the sense of the entire passage.

Contrary to expectation, Crabbe manages dialogue in the
relatively rigid couplet with surprising ease and flexibility.
Technically, of course, the very rigidity of the couplet allows
greater variation without destroying the pattern than would
otherwise be possible. We can readily illustrate how Crabbe
takes advantage of this situation. In "The Sisters" (*Tales*

of the Hall, Book VIII), Jane and Lucy are opposites in temperament, as the dialogue of their reactions to news of an absconding banker shows:

> " 'The odious villain!' Jane in wrath began;
> "In pity Lucy, 'The unhappy man!
> " 'When time and reason our affliction heal,
> " 'How will the author of our sufferings feel?'
> " 'And let him feel, my sister—let the woes
> " 'That he creates be bane to his repose!' "   (436-41)

In this passage two points are noteworthy: the natural division of the couplet at every other line is used to mark the change from one speaker to another, and in one instance the speakers change within the couplet itself. In "The Learned Boy" (*Tales,* No. XXI), widower Farmer Jones is being pursued by a widow with matrimonial intent:

> "Three girls," the widow cried, "a lively three
> "To govern well—indeed it cannot be."
> "Yes," he replied, "it calls for pains and care;
> "But I must bear it."—"Sir, you cannot bear;
> "Your son is weak, and asks a mother's eye."—
> "That, my kind friend, a father's may supply."—
> "Such growing griefs your very soul will tease."—
> "To grieve another would not give me ease;
> "I have a mother"—"She, poor ancient soul!
> "Can she the spirits of the young control?"   (41-50)

Here the dialogue changes at an even faster pace—not only between and within couplets, but within individual lines as well.

The foregoing characteristics reveal Crabbe's adaptation of the heroic couplet to narrative. His management of content and structure was equally successful. Criticism of the *Tales* and *Tales of the Hall* has usually taken the form of criticism of Crabbe as a didactic storyteller.[5] Little has there-

---

[5] In, for example, Alfred Ainger, *Crabbe,* pp. 91-146 and 163-84; and René Huchon, *George Crabbe and his Times,* trans. Frederick Clarke, pp. 316-73 and 403-31.

fore been said about his skill as a master of the short narrative. In the first place, although they do contain didactic interpolations, Crabbe's tales always make a strong appeal to the emotions, for they were intended primarily as entertainment.[6] Thus the opening of "The Confidant" (*Tales*, No. XVI) presents a strongly sympathetic picture of the heroine:

> Anna was young and lovely—in her eye
> The glance of beauty, in her cheek the dye;
> Her shape was slender, and her features small,
> But graceful, easy, unaffected all.
> The liveliest tints her youthful face disclosed;
> There beauty sparkled, and there health reposed;
> For the pure blood that flush'd that rosy cheek
> Spoke what the heart forbad the tongue to speak. (1-8)

And the following view of nature is charged with emotions that reflect those of the weak young hero in "Delay Has Danger"(*Tales of the Hall*, Book XIII):

> But now dejected, languid, listless, low,
> He saw the wind upon the water blow,
> And the cold stream curl'd onward as the gale
> From the pine-hill blew harshly down the dale.
> On the right side the youth a wood survey'd,
> With all its dark intensity of shade;
> Where the rough wind alone was heard to move,
> In this, the pause of nature and of love. (705-12)

In the context of the whole story, the sixth line ("With all its dark intensity of shade") is particularly successful.

[6] In the mature tales, Crabbe's main purpose was not didactic. Even as early as *The Parish Register*, his son contrasts it with his father's preceding poems by asserting that "in them there had been no tale—this was a chain of stories; they were didactic—here no moral inference is directly inculcated": *The Poetical Works of the Rev. George Crabbe*, ed. by his son, I, 184.

And in the Prefaces to the *Tales* and *Tales of the Hall*, Crabbe himself supports this view: "The first intention of the poet must be to please; for, if he means to instruct, he must render the instruction which he hopes to convey palatable and pleasant. I will not assume the tone of a moralist, nor promise that my relations shall be beneficial to mankind . . ." *Crabbe*, ed. Ward, II, 300.

Secondly, Crabbe understood[7] and put into practice many of the structural techniques of the short story. Most of his tales concentrate on a single climactic situation. In "Resentment" (*Tales*, No. XVII), for example, a stubborn obtuse woman carries revenge too far. Step by step, we follow her machinations until she finally relents—too late: her husband, the object of her revenge, is dead. The foreshortening of incidental materials to heighten the total effect is another structural device that Crabbe often makes use of. A somewhat extreme example appears in "The Widow's Tale" (*Tales*, No. VII). The widow, who has survived a loveless marriage, tells of the earlier tragedy of her real love. In search of fortune, the young man goes to sea, pursues his new career, and returns a failure—all in four lines!

> "From the rough ocean we beheld a gleam
> "Of joy, as transient as the joys we dream;
> "By lying hopes deceived, my friend retired,
> "And sail'd—was wounded—reach'd us—and expired!"
>
> (305-8)

The heightening of interest through foreshadowing is also a regular occurrence in the mature tales. Sometimes it is an obvious warning to the reader, as in "The Confidant," where the heroine, Anna, has confided the secret of her illegitimate child to her friend Eliza:

> The infant died; the face resumed each charm,
> And reason now brought trouble and alarm:
> "Should her Eliza—no! she was too just,
> "Too good and kind—but ah! too young to trust."
>
> (135-38)

At other times the foreshadowing is more subtle. In "The Mother," for example, a young parson is courting the daugh-

---

[7] In his tales, according to Crabbe, he set out to write "such composition as would possess a regular succession of events, and a catastrophe to which every incident should be subservient, and which every character, in a greater or less degree, should conspire to accomplish": *Crabbe*, ed. Ward, II, 6.

ter, Lucy, against her mother's wishes. She succeeds in creating the following situation, in which the last line hints at Lucy's subsequent disappointment and tragedy:

> Whate'er he wrote, he saw unread return'd,
> And he, indignant, the dishonour spurn'd;
> Nay, fix'd suspicion where he might confide,
> And sacrificed his passion to his pride.   (227-30)

The development of conflict through contrasts in character and situation is still another structural method used by Crabbe. Thus in "Advice, or The Squire and the Priest" (*Tales*, No. XV) a domineering worldly squire selects his young nephew as the rector of his village church on the assumption that he will be wholly compliant. The nephew's character is of course diametrically opposed to that of the uncle. In the end the young priest not only rejects the squire's "advice," but successfully challenges his authority. Contrasts in setting may be illustrated in "The Lover's Journey" (*Tales*, No. X). The young lover, on his way to an assignation, rides through scenes of squalor and ugliness, seeing in them nothing but beauty because he is happy; then, when the girl fails to meet him, he rides on through contrasting scenes of actual beauty, which now seem to him ugly and repulsive because he sees them with a jaundiced eye. There is in this situation an ingeniously worked out double contrast, psychologically in the young man and objectively in nature around him; and each side of the one is juxtaposed with the opposite side of the other.

A third way in which Crabbe's mastery of the short narrative reveals itself in the tales is in their emphasis upon character realistically interpreted. It is often Crabbe's practice to bring a character, with traits already indicated, into a crucial situation which dramatizes these traits. Thus in "The Brothers" (*Tales*, No. XX) we first learn of their contrasting natures:

> George was a bold, intrepid, careless lad,
> With just the failings that his father had;
> Isaac was weak, attentive, slow, exact,
> With just the virtues that his father lack'd. (11-14)

As the story proceeds, these characteristics slowly flower in the lives of the two men. George, a sailor carelessly generous, aids his brother time and again. Isaac, accepting this aid, selfishly gives nothing but advice in return. Then comes the crucial situation. George loses his leg at sea, but confidently looks to Isaac, now rich and happily married, to take him in. This test Isaac fails to meet, thus revealing his true character or lack of it.

Like "The Brothers," the majority of Crabbe's tales are studies of character placed in situations which reveal strength or weakness. One of the best of these is "Procrastination" (*Tales,* No. IV), a study of the disintegrating effects of delay on character and on love. The subject seems to have interested Crabbe greatly, for he used it again as one of the *Tales of the Hall,* "Delay Has Danger," in which the delay reveals the weakness of the man in succumbing to the charms of another woman. In "Procrastination," however, the delay involves the girl, Dinah, who, separated from her lover Rupert, gradually succumbs to her wealthy aunt's love of riches and finery.

The tale is divisible into three parts, the first of which is introductory exposition, leading up to Rupert's going abroad to seek his fortune. Given the lovers, Dinah and Rupert, we are soon introduced to the major complication—the fact that the girl is living with and dependent upon her wealthy aunt and that the young man is similarly dependent upon his father. There is in addition a strong hint about their future:

> A wealthy aunt her gentle niece sustain'd,
> He, with a father, at his desk remain'd;

> The youthful couple, to their vows sincere,
> Thus loved expectant; year succeeding year,
> With pleasant views and hopes, but not a prospect near.
>
> (17-21)

The aunt is sickly and opposes the marriage, promising the lovers her estate when she dies. Soon it appears, however, that she has no intention of dying and that she selfishly wants Dinah unmarried as "servant, and nurse, and comforter, and friend." Finally, after many years, Rupert has a chance to go abroad to make his fortune. The lovers' parting foreshadows the outcome, emphasizing the gloom and uncertainty of their situation, with an ironic reference to Dinah's "too certain" future:

> The lovers parted with a gloomy view,
> And little comfort but that both were true;
> He for uncertain duties doom'd to steer,
> While hers remain'd too certain and severe.   (62-65)

Upon this note the first part ends.

In Part II we witness the stages of the slow shift from Dinah's love for Rupert to her love for wealth and finery; midway in the process "love of treasure had as large a part, As love of Rupert, in the virgin's heart." But the change did not occur without a struggle:

> Sometimes the past would on her mind intrude,
> And then a conflict full of care ensued;
> The thoughts of Rupert on her mind would press,
> His worth she knew, but doubted his success.   (126-29)

Finally, however, Dinah seems to be wholly converted to a love of wealth:

> For she indulged, nor was her heart so small,
> That one strong passion should engross it all.
> A love of splendour now with av'rice strove,
> And oft appear'd to be the stronger love.

. . . . .

> While books devout were near her—to destroy,
> Should it arise, an overflow of joy.   (144-57)

The last couplet is a subtle hint about the outcome, when
Dinah will pretend a consecration to religion in order to put
off the returned Rupert. The aunt having died at last and
left everything to her, Dinah is free to indulge her new pas-
sion for splendor. What she has now become is symbolized
in the luxurious details of her apartment:

> Within the fair apartment, guests might see
> The comforts cull'd for wealth by vanity.
> Around the room an Indian paper blazed,
> With lively tint and figures boldly raised;
> Silky and soft upon the floor below,
> Th' elastic carpet rose with crimson glow;
> All things around implied both cost and care;
> What met the eye was elegant or rare.
> Some curious trifles round the room were laid,
> By hope presented to the wealthy maid:
> Within a costly case of varnish'd wood,
> In level rows, her polish'd volumes stood;
> Shown as a favour to a chosen few,
> To prove what beauty for a book could do;
> A silver urn with curious work was fraught;
> A silver lamp from Grecian pattern wrought:
> Above her head, all gorgeous to behold,
> A time-piece stood on feet of burnish'd gold . . .
>   (158-75)

Dinah's transformation, however, is not as complete as it
seems, for next we are shown that her conscience still troubles
her. As she sits in her gorgeous apartment, two friends drop
in to gossip about these "degen'rate times": they conclude
that "What was once our pride is now our shame":

> Dinah was musing, as her friends discoursed,
> When these last words a sudden entrance forced
> Upon her mind, and what was once her pride

And now her shame, some painful views supplied;
Thoughts of the past within her bosom press'd,
And there a change was felt, and was confess'd.

(190-95)

Although Dinah has outwardly succumbed to her love of
luxury, an inner struggle remains to make the final outcome
uncertain. Thus suspense is maintained, and as Part III
opens with the dramatic reappearance of Rupert in this gor-
geous apartment, we await the climax of the story.

Part III arises ingeniously out of Part II. A maid in-
terrupts Dinah and her friends with the excited announce-
ment that "A huge tall sailor, with his tawny cheek, And
pitted face, will with my lady speak." Dinah receives the
news "trembling and distress'd" and "by her fears oppress'd."
At Rupert's first words, however, we see her for what she has
become; the truth appears in the poet's cool and ironic
comment:

Meantime the prudent Dinah had contrived
Her soul to question, and she then revived. (218-19)

The climax follows quickly when, in response to Rupert's
warm and anxious offer of love and marriage, Dinah rejects
him, hypocritically giving religion and her advanced age as
the reasons. That Dinah is sensitive about her wealth and
what it has done to her, we learn from her quick response to
Rupert's remark that "time has left us something to enjoy,"
which for him is not a reference to her money:

"What! thou hast learn'd my fortune?—yes, I live
"To feel how poor the comforts wealth can give;
"Thou too perhaps art wealthy; but our fate
"Still mocks our wishes, wealth is come too late."

(231-34)

To every argument that Rupert advances, Dinah has a firm,
if insincere, reply; finally the man gives up:

Proud and indignant, suffering, sick and poor,
He grieved unseen, and spoke of love no more—
Till all he felt in indignation died,
As hers had sunk in avarice and pride.   (300-3)

This is the note on which the story ends, but the poet continues for fifty more lines to emphasize and elaborate the tragedy of character—particularly Dinah's. The concluding paragraph shows Dinah at her lowest and worst. While on a shopping trip, she passes Rupert, who watches her "as if to find What were the movements of that subtle mind":

But Dinah moves—she had observed before
The pensive Rupert at an humble door.
Some thoughts of pity raised by his distress,
Some feeling touch of ancient tenderness;
Religion, duty, urged the maid to speak
In terms of kindness to a man so weak;
But pride forbad, and to return would prove
She felt the shame of his neglected love;
Nor wrapp'd in silence could she pass, afraid
Each eye should see her, and each heart upbraid.
One way remain'd—the way the Levite took,
Who without mercy could on misery look,
(A way perceived by craft, approved by pride):
She cross'd, and pass'd him on the other side.[8]

In addition to what has been noted already, this story of "character" succeeds as narrative fiction because its people are never merely symbols of moral abstractions. Their world is not the black-and-white world of right and wrong: it is the actual world with infinite mixtures of the two, in which these people live as complex human beings. Although he is more sinned against than sinning, Rupert is weak; he partially forfeits our sympathy by his failures before going abroad and by his oversimplified demands on his return.

---

[8] "This is the end of *Procrastination,* a tale of slow moral decay and of disillusionment, theme and effect being such as are commonly sought by modern practitioners of the 'art of the short-story' ": Leavis, *op. cit.,* pp. 127-28.

Dinah, although acting despicably at the end, nevertheless feels "Some thought of pity raised by his distress, Some feeling touch of ancient tenderness." There is a genuine struggle within her, finally resolved in favor of the baser side of her nature, the growth of which has been the theme of the story. But of the three elements of this baser nature—pride, fear, and shame—the last two reveal the operation of a guilty conscience.

Not all of Crabbe's successful tales emphasize character as strongly as does "Procastination." Again like the short story, some of them depend primarily upon situation. Of these "The Frank Courtship" is an excellent example. Unlike the tales of pathos and grim reality commonly associated with Crabbe, "The Frank Courtship" is almost Chaucerian in its humorous vitality. And as is usual with Crabbe at his best, the structure and dialogue in couplet form are precise and sure.

The story concerns the attempts of a pious domineering father to dictate the marriage of his clever and beautiful daughter. As we shall see, however, the situation is by no means this simple, for paradoxically both father and daughter have their way in the end. The poem opens with emphasis upon the father:

> Grave Jonas Kindred, Sybil Kindred's sire,
> Was six feet high, and look'd six inches higher;
>
> .   .   .   .   .
>
> Himself he view'd with undisguised respect,
> And never pardon'd freedom or neglect.   (1-14)

Although the mother is completely dominated by Jonas, the daughter, we soon learn, is not; for "Sooth'd by attention from her early years, She gain'd all wishes by her smiles or tears." The remainder of the introduction (the first seventy-eight lines) rounds out the setting in which Sybil grows up. In the home, for example, "each table, chair, and stool, Stood in its place, or moving moved by rule."

The story itself begins with the request by Jonas' widowed sister for Sybil as a companion. The father accedes to the request, not knowing that the girl's aunt, who lives in another town, will introduce her to a life of luxury:

> All here was gay and cheerful—all at home
> Unvaried quiet and unruffled gloom.
> There were no changes, and amusements few;
> Here, all was varied, wonderful, and new;
> There were plain meals, plain dresses, and grave looks—
> Here, gay companions and amusing books;
> And the young beauty soon began to taste
> The light vocations of the scene she graced.   (101-8)

This situation is precisely that of Dinah with her aunt in "Procastination," except that Sybil, a stronger character, enjoys the life of luxury without being overwhelmed by it. Even when she joins her aunt in deceiving her father about her new way of life, Sybil, we remember, is merely continuing her childhood habit of having her own way. However, lest we rashly conclude that she is slipping, the author tells us, with another hint of foreshadowing, that Sybil,

> . . . fond of pleasure, gay and light,
> Had still a secret bias to the right;
> Vain as she was—and flattery made her vain—
> Her simulation gave her bosom pain.   (133-36)

At this point the major complication is introduced—we meet the hero, Josiah, whom Sybil's father has selected as her future husband: "Sober he was and grave from early youth, Mindful of forms, but more intent on truth." After three years with her aunt, Sybil is ordered home to meet the young man. What she will do in this crisis and how she feels about her aunt's way of life are now made clear:

> But would not Sybil to the matron cling,
> And fear to leave the shelter of her wing?
> No! in the young there lives a love of change,

> And to the easy they prefer the strange!
> Then too the joys she once pursued with zeal,
> From whist and visits sprung, she ceased to feel.
>
> (188-93)

Once she is back home, Sybil at first delights and then disappoints her father, who rather quaintly reproaches the aunt—she "has by her arts defiled The ductile spirit of my darling child." Jonas sternly warns his daughter against rejecting the chosen suitor. To this warning Sybil retorts that her aunt "will with pride protect One whom a father can for this reject." Jonas throws up his hands in despair, and leaves Sybil to her mother. Then follows an amusing scene in which the girl, her head filled with the romances her aunt has let her read, announces her standards for a lover:

> "I must be loved," said Sybil; "I must see
> "The man in terrors who aspires to me;
> "At my forbidding frown his heart must ache,
> "His tongue must falter, and his frame must shake;
> "And, if I grant him at my feet to kneel,
> "What trembling, fearful pleasure must he feel;
> "Nay, such the raptures that my smiles inspire,
> "That reason's self must for a time retire."

To which her mother replies:

> "Alas! for good Josiah. . . .
> "These wicked thoughts would fill his soul with shame.
> "He kneel and tremble at a thing of dust!
> "He cannot, child."—The child replied, "He must."
>
> (294-305)

In addition to the humor and mild satire of this passage, the masterful handling of dialogue within the couplet form is noteworthy. The virtues of the couplet are here exploited to their fullest in the service of narration, and the result is a compact, dramatic, fast-moving scene.

As the climax of the story approaches—the "fatal interview" between Sybil and Josiah—all forces seem arrayed against her, and she appears adamant:

> "Nothing shall tempt, shall force me to bestow
> "My hand upon him—yet I wish to know."   (329-30)

The qualification in the last clause, however, makes possible the denouement. Their meeting reveals the two as antagonists by preparation, but they also see and sense much to admire in each other: incipient love at first sight clashes with strong previously held attitudes, which neither will forego in the presence of the other. In this scene of sparkling comedy, Sybil and Josiah first gaze at each other in silence until silence becomes embarrassing. Finally Josiah speaks in a vein that Sybil quickly and cleverly takes up:

> . . . "Fair maiden, art thou well?"—
> "Art thou physician?" she replied; "my hand,
> "My pulse, at least, shall be at thy command."
>   (367-69)

Then in a mock doctor–patient relationship they frankly appraise and criticize one another. At last Josiah tries to introduce the serious reason for his visit, only to be haughtily rebuffed by the girl:

> "True, lovely Sybil; and, this point agreed,
> "Let me to those of greater weight proceed:
> "Thy father!"—"Nay," she quickly interposed,
> "Good doctor, here our conference is closed!"
>   (446-49)

When the father learns what has happened, he senses that Josiah is smitten, and he is furious at Sybil's response. In the final scene of the story, father and daughter meet in a lively dialogue that completes the revelation of Sybil's character and humorously resolves her father's dilemma:

> "Couldst thou his pure and modest mind distress,
> "By vile remarks upon his speech, address,

"Attire, and voice?"—"All this I must confess."—
"Unhappy child! what labour will it cost
"To win him back!"—"I do not think him lost."—
"Courts he then, trifler, insult and disdain?"—
"No: but from these he courts me to refrain."—
"Then hear me, Sybil: should Josiah leave
"Thy father's house?"—"My father's child would grieve."—
"That is of grace; and if he come again
"To speak of love?"—"I might from grief refrain."—
"Then wilt thou, daughter, our design embrace?"—
"Can I resist it, if it be of grace?"—
"Dear child! in three plain words thy mind express —
"Wilt thou have this good youth?"—"Dear father! yes."

In "The Frank Courtship," as in "Procastination," we are in the real world of lights and shades. The character of Sybil is extremely complex, as revealed particularly in the scenes with her lover and her father at the end. Even Josiah, who appears late in the story, is made thoroughly human by a number of quick insights into his character—such as his response to the father's advice that he dominate the forthcoming interview with Sybil:

> A sober smile return'd the youth, and said,
> "Can I cause fear, who am myself afraid?" (325-26)

And old imperious Jonas himself becomes sympathetic and likable when he meets his match in his versatile and talented daughter.

There are not many today who would echo a critic's recent comment on Crabbe, "that he is (or ought to be—for who reads him?) a living classic."[9] The decline of Crabbe's reputation in the nineteenth century is of course understandable. Far more genuinely than Byron, he defended the Augustan tradition by precept and practice at a time when Shelley and Keats were doing some of their best work. Yet the arch-

[9] Leavis, *op. cit.*, p. 125.

romantic Scott was one of Crabbe's most enthusiastic admirers, and Charles Lamb dramatized one of his *Tales* ("The Confidant")! Unquestionably Crabbe had something to offer which transcended these labels. For us today that something lies both in the fact that he was the last of the Augustans and that, in his best work, he brilliantly adapted the heroic couplet to the art of narrative.

Chapter VIII

Epilogue to the Succession

THE WORK of the later masters of the heroic couplet covers more than a century of literary history and an astonishing variety of subject matter. And the treatment of that subject matter itself varies from the powerful satire of Johnson and Churchill to the humorous or pathetic narratives of Crabbe. Viewed as part of the two hundred-year-old tradition of the heroic couplet, the work of these five poets constitutes, roughly, the second half of that tradition. As such, their significance is approximately equal to that of Dryden and Pope together, although in originality, individual importance, and sheer genius, no one of them compares with either Dryden or Pope. For, as we said at the beginning of this study, all five later masters derive from and exploit parts of the tradition as established before them. They modified the tradition in the process of conforming to it. Consequently their work—the poetry of Gay, Johnson, Churchill, Goldsmith, and Crabbe—attained a permanence that makes it still enjoyable and worth studying, even though the tradition of which it is a vital part is no longer operative.

The full-fledged heroic couplet died with Crabbe, the last of the masters of the form. Keats's *Lamia*, written distantly in the Dryden manner, appeared in 1820; but *Lamia* is technically a transition poem and is therefore not creatively in the tradition. In fact, Keats's *Endymion*, published in the year before Crabbe's *Tales of the Hall* (1819), is equally important for the light it throws upon the status of the pentameter couplet, the general nature of which reveals why at this time the heroic couplet lost its traditional vitality.[1]

At the turn of the nineteenth century many poets continued to use the heroic couplet, but, except for Crabbe, they did nothing that had not been done much better by their neo-classic predecessors. Some of these poets were, however, among the most popular of their time, although, with one exception (Byron), they were forgotten in the later recognition of the "romantic revolt." They include Samuel Rogers (*The Pleasures of Memory*, 1792), Robert Bloomfield (*The Farmer's Boy*, 1798), Thomas Campbell (*The Pleasures of Hope*, 1799), and Byron, (*English Bards and Scots Reviewers*, 1809).

The heroic-couplet poems of Rogers, Bloomfield, and Campbell are manifestly second-rate, if not worse; yet even in their inferior treatment of subject matter they employ many of the metrical and syntactic characteristics of the traditional form—but with too mechanical and lifeless a regularity. In addition, such devices as personification and apostrophe, used sparingly by the later masters of the heroic couplet, are here used to excess. Thus within eighty lines near the beginning of Campbell's *Pleasures of Hope* (45-121) personified "Hope" is apostrophized as "Auspicious Hope! . . . Angel of life! . . . Friend of the brave! . . . Congenial Hope!"—each time followed by a long passage of trite and sentimental moralizing. Byron's satire, on the other hand, still retains much of its original flavor and gusto. Although it was admittedly written in imitation of Dryden and Pope and its couplets are technically a forceful amalgamation of both, there are also a typically Byronic impulsiveness within the lines and a flair for experimentation with rhyme that are not neo-classic.

[1] For a critical analysis of the Keats pentameter couplet, see Walter Jackson Bate, *The Stylistic Development of Keats*, pp. 19-42 and 146-71.

Among the critics of the time the now-recognized major figures (Coleridge, Hazlitt, Lamb, and De Quincey) were all opposed to the heroic couplet, but the most popular and influential contemporary critics were its supporters: Jeffrey, Wilson, Croker, Lockhart, Byron, etc. With the exception of Byron, they too are now almost forgotten men, but their attacks on the Keats and Leigh Hunt couplet were destructive enough to start the false rumor that they had literally killed Keats. We are here concerned not so much with the validity of these critical views as with the fact that they represent one side of a sustained controversy over the nature of the pentameter couplet.

In their criticism of Keats's *Endymion*, Lockhart and Croker broadly defend the neo-classic tradition and specifically measure the Keats couplet against the earlier heroic couplet. Thus Lockart says:

Having cooled a little from this "fine passion," our youthful poet passes very naturally into a long strain of foaming abuse against a certain class of English poets whom, with Pope at their head, it is much the fashion with the ignorant unsettled pretenders of the present time to undervalue.[2]

To which we may add Byron's general assertion that "there can be no worse sign for the taste of the time than the depreciation of Pope."[3] Croker takes up the more detailed analysis:

There is hardly a complete couplet enclosing a complete idea in the whole book. He wanders from one subject to another, from the association, not of the ideas but of sounds, and the work is composed of hemistichs which, it is quite evident, have forced themselves upon the author by the mere force of the catchwords on which they turn. . . . We come now to the author's taste in versification. He cannot indeed write a sentence, but perhaps he may be able to spin a line. Let us see. The following are specimens of his prosodial notions of our English heroic metre.[4]

[2] "The Cockney School of Poetry," *Blackwood's Edinburgh Magazine*, III, 520.
[3] *The Works of Lord Byron*, ed. R. E. Prothero, V, 559.
[4] "Endymion: A Poetic Romance," *The Quarterly Review*, XIX, 206-7.

And Lockhart is even more specific about the poetic form of
Endymion:

Before giving any extracts, we must inform our readers that this
romance is meant to be written in English heroic rhyme.   To
those who have read any of Hunt's poems, this hint might indeed
be needless.   Mr. Keats has adopted the loose, nerveless versifi-
cation, and Cockney rhymes of the poet of *Rimini.*[5]

Clearly "the loose, nerveless versification, and Cockney
rhymes" describe a couplet in which distinctness of form
(end-stopped in thought, parallel in syntax) and clarity of
rhyme (emphatic and significant) are conspicuously absent.
    On the other side of this controversy, Leigh Hunt's at-
tack on the heroic couplet represents the forces of revolt
aimed at discrediting a traditional verse form.   In his remarks
on variety versus monotony in versification, Hunt declares
that,

Variety in versification consists in whatsoever can be done for the
prevention of monotony, by diversity of stops and cadences, dis-
tribution of emphasis, and retardation and acceleration of time;
for the whole real secret of versification is a musical secret, and
is not attainable to any vital effect save by the ear of genius. . . .
The same time and quantity which are occasioned by the spiritual
part of this secret, thus become its formal ones—not feet and
syllables, long and short, iambics or trochees; which are the re-
duction of it to its *less* than dry bones.   You might get, for
instance, not only ten and eleven, but thirteen or fourteen syllables
into a riming, as well as blank heroical verse, if time and feeling
permitted. . . .[6]

Here in principle is a rejection of the major characteristics
of the heroic couplet.   Hunt quotes twelve lines from Pope's
Rape of the Lock (II, 7-18) as an example of monotony in
versification, with the following comment:

[5] *Op. cit.,* p. 522.
[6] Leigh Hunt, *An Answer to the Question, 'What is Poetry,'* pp. 51-52.

The reader will observe that it is literally *see-saw*, like the rising and falling of a plank, with a light person at one end who is jerked up on the briefer time, and a heavier one who is set down more leisurely at the other.[7]

Hunt's entire objection to this passage rests upon the fact that the caesura occurs after the fourth syllable of every line, a practice unusual for so many consecutive lines even in Pope. And in making this criticism, Hunt ignores the other sources of variety in the passage, such as trochaic and pyrrhic substitution (in lines 7, 8, 10, 11, 12, 13, 17, and 18) and the suppression of one stress in lines 8 and 10.

It is also worth noting that the preceding and following passages from *The Rape of the Lock* are not open to the objection that Hunt makes to the passage he has selected. In the preceding six lines the caesura occurs after the fourth, fifth, or sixth syllable, the order being: 5, 5, 4, 5, 6, 4; and in the ten lines which follow Hunt's passage the variations are so extreme that they violate Pope's own formula for the medial caesura! The major pauses in this passage occur after the following syllables: 2nd, 4th, 4th, 5th, 6th, 4th, 5th, 4th, 3rd, and 5th.

Apart from his faulty scansion of Pope, Hunt's principles (not bad in themselves) provide justification for some kind of non-heroic couplet. But the extremes to which he and Keats go in *The Story of Rimini* and *Endymion* could only result in inferior poetry and the breakdown of the pentameter couplet as a distinct poetic form. Keats himself realized this, and a year later, in *Lamia*, he brought order out of the chaos of his earlier couplets. What Keats did was to recognize a basic principle about poetic form (which Hunt, for all his own fine principles, did not)—the principle involving pattern versus variation: unless the pattern remains distinct in the background, the variations will destroy it.

An analysis of representative passages from *Endymion*

7 *Ibid.,* p. 53.

and *The Story of Rimini* will reveal the extent of the dis-
integration of poetic form in these poems. From *Endymion*,
consider the following:

> Young companies nimbly began dancing,
> To the swift treble pipe, and humming string.
> Aye, those fair living forms swam heavenly
> To tunes forgotten—out of memory:
> Fair creatures! whose young children's children bred
> Thermopylae its heroes—not yet dead,
> But in old marbles ever beautiful.
> High genitors, unconscious did they cull
> Time's sweet first-fruits—they danced to weariness,
> And then in quiet circles did they press
> The hillock turf, and caught the latter end
> Of some strange history, potent to send
> A young mind from its bodily tenement.
> Or they might watch the quoit-pitchers, intent
> On either side . . .   (I, 313-27)

The second half of this passage is predominantly enjambed,
but this in itself does not necessarily weaken or destroy the
couplet pattern. In fact, as couplets the first half is inferior
to the second. The chief weakness is in the rhymes, which
are not even respectably feminine. The normal accent in
three out of these four pairs of rhymes is completely ig-
nored ("danc*ing*"–"*string*," "heaven*ly*"–"mem*ory*," "beauti-
ful"–"*cull*"), a fact which cancels out their importance in
meaning as rhyme words. Indeed, in these instances we may
say that rhyme almost ceases to exist. Related to this neglect
of normal accent is the metrical chaos of three of the lines
and the too-frequent interruption of the pattern throughout
the passage. The rhythms of the following lines cannot, by
any stretch of the imagination, be called poetic in terms of
the iambic pattern of the whole poem:

> Young companies nimbly began dancing . . .
> Of some strange history, potent to send . . .
> Or they might watch the quoit-pitchers, intent . . .

This is indeed not poetic composition, but poetic decomposition!

The same "loose, nerveless versification, and Cockney rhymes" characterize *The Story of Rimini*, of which the following passage describing Francesca's beautiful summerhouse, where the lovers meet, is typical:

> And on a line with this ran round about
> A like relief, touched exquisitely out,
> That shewed, in various scenes, the nymphs themselves;
> Some by the water side on bowery shelves
> Leaning at will,—some in the water sporting
> With sides half swelling forth, and looks of courting,—
> Some in a flowery dell, hearing a swain
> Play on his pipe, till the hills ring again,—
> Some tying up their long moist hair,—some sleeping
> Under the trees, with fauns and satyrs peeping,—
> Or, sidelong-eyed, pretending not to see
> The latter in the brakes come creepingly,
> While their forgotten urns, lying about
> In the green herbage, let the water out.   (III, 470-83)

The rhymes, although maintaining the couplet pattern, are relatively weak and uncertain. Only two of the seven couplets have emphatic and significant rhyme words ("themselves"–"shelves" and "swain"–"again"). The others are either feminine rhymes, ending on unstressed syllables, or they are unimportant in meaning or the normal accent is ignored ("sporting"–"courting," "sleeping"–"creeping." "about"–"out" and *see*–"creeping*ly*"). But far more damaging to the metrical pattern are the too-frequent and irregular interruptions of the iambic norm. The result is the intrusion of essentially prose rhythms into the poetic line, in such an instance as the following:

> Some in a flowery dell, hearing a swain
> Play on his pipe, till the hills ring again . . .

This practice almost blurs the iambic pattern out of existence. In addition to metrical weakness, there are a syntactic looseness and a tendency toward verbiage which consign the passage (as well as the whole poem) to poetic mediocrity. Hunt's quest for variety in versification (consisting "in whatsoever can be done for the prevention of monotony, by diversity of stops and cadences, distribution of emphasis, and retardation and acceleration of time") led him too often into metrical chaos; but the principle which he espoused was put to better practice by his contemporaries.

The generally hostile attitude of the Romantic critics towards neo-classicism naturally implicated the heroic couplet. Hunt's more specific attacks on the form indicated a possible alternative, with which he and Keats first experimented unsuccessfully. But Keats later, and Tom Moore and Shelley in particular, evolved a kind of compromise couplet that retained its form (at a distance) and that also pointed the way to the superficial retention of the form without any of the spirit in such a poem as Browning's *My Last Duchess*. We may say, therefore, that the so-called enjambed or run-on couplet appears to best advantage in the work of Moore, Keats, and Shelley. Technically it represents a loosening, a relaxing, of the form in the direction of blank verse. The caesura may occur almost anywhere—or not at all. Metrical substitution becomes more frequent. In meaning and stress, the rhymes tend to be de-emphasized. And, most important of all, the syntax becomes dominantly oblique rather than parallel, so that balance and antithesis are the exception rather than the rule. The dominance of these characteristics represents a final step in the decline of the heroic couplet.

Moore's handling of the run-on couplet is most typical in the first part of *Lalla Rookh*, subtitled "The Veiled Prophet of Khorassan." Consider, for example, the following passage:

> Sad and subdued, for the first time her frame
> Trembled with horror, when the summons came
> (A summons proud and rare, which all but she,
> And she, till now, had heard with ecstasy)
> To meet Mokanna at his place of prayer,
> A garden oratory, cool and fair,
> By the stream's side, where still at close of day
> The Prophet of the Veil retired to pray;
> Sometimes alone—but, oftener far, with one,
> One chosen nymph to share his orison.

Here the rhymes are all masculine and the rhyme words convey significant meaning. They all maintain normal accent except "ecstasy" and "orison," in which the final syllable is a half stress. All the lines are either four- or five-stress, and the caesura varies from the fourth to the seventh syllable. The first four couplets are enjambed, but the couplet pattern is not blurred beyond recognition. The thought of the first couplet runs on to the third ("when the summons came . . . To meet Mokanna"), but the parenthetical second couplet reaffirms the pattern, and there are no full stops within the lines. Although there is considerable metrical substitution (especially in the first, second, fifth, sixth, and eighth lines), the iambic pattern is always clearly in the background. Finally, the syntax is forward-moving (oblique), with occasional interruptions that are digressive but not parallel.

Even, in exceptional instances, when Moore does use parallel structure, the accompanying enjambment creates effects that are not those of the heroic couplet:

> And such was now young Zelica—so changed
> From her who, some years since, delighted ranged
> The almond groves that shade Bokhara's tide,
> All life and bliss, with Azim by her side!
> So altered was she now, this festal day,
> When, 'mid the proud Divan's dazzling array,
> The vision of that Youth whom she had loved,

> Had wept as dead, before her breathed and moved;
> When—bright, she thought, as if from Eden's track
> But half-way trodden, he had wandered back
> Again to earth, glistening with Eden's light—
> Her beauteous Azim shone before her sight.

The parallelism is signalized by the "so changed," "So altered," "When," and "When" constructions. But all is not parallel, for the first "so" occurs at the end, and the second "So" at the beginning, of a line; and although the two "when's" appear first in their lines, one of them is in the second line of its couplet and the other in the first. Furthermore, the second "When" grammatically introduces a clause that is three lines away ("When . . . Her beauteous Azim shone before her sight"), being thus widely separated by the three-line enjambed clause within the dashes.

In *Lamia*, despite Keats's preliminary study of Dryden, the couplet is more relaxed than it is in *Lalla Rookh*. The following passage will indicate the difference:

> For the first time, since first he harbour'd in
> That purple-lined palace of sweet sin,
> His spirit pass'd beyond its golden bourne
> Into the noisy world almost forsworn.
> The lady, ever watchful, penetrant,
> Saw this with pain, so arguing a want
> Of something more, more than her empery
> Of joys; and she began to moan and sigh
> Because he mused beyond her, knowing well
> That but a moment's thought is passion's passing bell.
>
> (II, 30-39)

There is here a good deal of freedom, but the couplet pattern remains distinct in the background, as it too often does not in *Endymion*. Three of the rhyme words are either insignificant in meaning or are artificially stressed on their last syllables ("in," "penetrant," and "empery"), but there are no feminine rhymes. There is considerable metrical substitu-

tion (in lines 1, 2, 4, 6, and 7); the lines are predominantly
five-stress, with two four-stress and the concluding hexame-
ter; and the caesura is relatively free, varying from the
second to the seventh syllable. Finally, the syntax is en-
tirely forward-moving, with no parallelism whatsoever. Else-
where enjambment and freedom of caesura are even more
pronounced, as in the following couplets:

> Fine was the mitigated fury, like
> Apollo's presence when in act to strike
> The serpent—Ha, the serpent! certes, she
> Was none. She burnt, she loved the tyranny,
> And, all subdued, consented to the hour
> When to the bridal he should lead his paramour.
>
> (II, 78-83)

The interruptions of the thought within lines (full stops and
exclamations), the caesura moving from the second to the
ninth syllable, the de-emphasized rhymes—all combine to
give a run-on effect to the whole passage.

Shelley's management of the couplet, like that of Keats,
is relaxed; but his metrical pattern is more firm and precise.
Although his earlier "conversation," *Julian and Maddalo*,
is technically interesting, *Epipsychidion* probably represents
his best performance in this form. From it we may consider
the following passage:

> Love is like understanding, that grows bright,
> Gazing on many truths; 'tis like thy light,
> Imagination! which from earth and sky,
> And from the depths of human fantasy,
> As from a thousand prisms and mirrors, fills
> The Universe with glorious beams, and kills
> Error, the worm, with many a sun-like arrow
> Of its reverberated lightning. Narrow
> The heart that loves, the brain that contemplates,
> The life that wears, the spirit that creates
> One object, and one form, and builds thereby
> A sepulchre for its eternity.   (162-73)

This is the run-on couplet at its best. The lines are all four-
or five-stress; but the caesura is much freer, varying from
none at all (in the last line) to the ninth syllable (in line 5).
Half the couplets are wholly enjambed, and none is com-
pletely end-stopped: except for the end of the passage, all
full stops occur within the lines. One couplet has feminine
rhymes ("arrow"–"narrow"), and two require a forced ac-
cent on the last syllable ("sky"–"fantasy" and "thereby"–
"eternity"). The syntax is oblique, except for the last sen-
tence, which is structurally a parallel series; but this paral-
lelism does not coincide with the couplet structure, as it
would in the heroic couplet. Its movement is opposed to
that of the metrical pattern, a relationship that may be de-
scribed as a kind of counterpoint.

This sampling of couplet poems by Moore, Keats, and
Shelley is not, of course, exhaustive; nor is it intended to
evaluate, absolutely or by comparison, their poems as wholes.
What we have done is to illustrate the nature of the run-on
pentameter couplet at precisely the time when the life of the
heroic couplet was drawing to a close (1817-21). The run-on
couplet may be further described as marking a halfway point
between the heroic couplet and blank verse. It retains the
couplet pattern, but the characteristics peculiar to that pat-
tern are so relaxed by variations that they threaten to destroy
the pattern itself. To put the matter another way, the quali-
ties of the couplet tend to become mere decoration, not es-
sential to the poetic form. When this process is completed,
we have what amounts to blank verse with decorative rhymes
in pairs. It seems to me that this situation obtains in Brown-
ing's *My Last Duchess,* for reasons that we may now briefly
consider.

It is not irrelevant to remark that probably most people
do not think of *My Last Duchess* as a poem in couplets. In
my own experience, the great majority of students who study
the poem tend not to notice the couplet rhymes unless their

attention is called to them; and in memory they associate its poetic form with that of Browning's other great dramatic monologues, which is of course blank verse. There is, I believe, good reason for these tendencies. The rhymes in *My Last Duchess* are more casual in meaning, emphasis, and structural form than those of any of the poems we have noted except *Endymion* and *The Story of Rimini*. At the risk of committing a sacrilege, I shall quote the first twelve lines of the poem with the rhymes eliminated by making one change in each couplet:

> That's my last Duchess painted on the wall,
> Looking as if she were alive. I hold
> That piece a wonder, now: Fra Pandolf's brush
> Worked busily a day, and there she stands.
> Will't please you sit and look at her? I said
> "Fra Pandolf" by design, for never saw
> Strangers like you that pictured countenance,
> The depth and passion of its earnest look,
> But to myself they turned (since none puts by
> The curtain I have drawn for you, but me)
> And seemed as they would ask me, if they dared,
> How such a glance came there; so, not the first
> Are you to turn and ask thus.

The six substitutions are as follows: "hold" for "call," "brush" for "hands," "saw" for "read," "look" for "glance," "me" for "I," and "dared" for "durst." With the possible exception of the "saw" for "read" (past tense), these changes alter the original meaning very little; and in two of the six there is not only no change at all ("me" for "I" and "dared" for "durst"), but in one an improvement in Browning's grammar!

The almost complete enjambment of the couplets reduces rhyme emphasis to a very low point. The rhymes therefore become relatively unimportant and can be eliminated without seriously distorting the verse form. Within the passage,

only one out of four full stops occurs at the end of a line
(for the whole poem the comparable figures are six out of
thirty-one).   Metrically the lines are all four- or five-stress,
but the caesura is relatively free, varying from the fourth to
the eighth syllable.   The syntax is nonparallel, or entirely
oblique.   With these considerations in mind, I believe that
we may describe *My Last Duchess* structurally as a blank
verse poem with incidental rhyme.

With imitative exceptions, the pentameter couplet never
afterwards became anything more than the run-on form.
The closed heroic couplet, with its limited caesura and num-
ber of stresses per line, its emphatic rhymes, its coincidence
of thought and couplet unit, and, above all, its predominantly
parallel syntax—that couplet did not appear again.   And
today, although some critical interest in this form has ap-
peared (mainly in the work of Eliot and Winters), there has
been no important revival of it.   Indeed it is significant that
when Allen Tate wrote a poem on Alexander Pope, he used
quatrains.   And Eliot's experiment with heroic couplets was
not, according to him, a success:

I remember that Pound once induced me to destroy what I
thought an excellent set of couplets; for, said he, "Pope has done
this so well that you cannot do it better; and if you mean this as
a burlesque, you had better suppress it, for you cannot parody
Pope unless you can write better verse than Pope—and you
can't."[8]

With the critical implications of this incident, we may well
conclude our study of the later masters of the heroic couplet,
particulary if we remember Eliot's further admonition that
"the sad ghost of Coleridge beckons to me from the shadows."

[8] *Ezra Pound: Selected Poems*, ed. T. S. Eliot, p. xxi.

A Selected Bibliography

The following books and articles have been quoted from or otherwise directly referred to in this study:

BOOKS

Addison, Joseph. *The Spectator.* Edited by G. Gregory Smith. London, 1897.

Ainger, Alfred. *Crabbe.* New York, 1903.

Aubin, R. A., *Topographical Poetry in XVIII-Century England.* New York, 1936.

Bate, Walter J. *The Stylistic Development of Keats.* New York, 1945.

Bloomfield, Robert. *The Farmer's Boy.* London, 1800.

Brooks, Cleanth. *The Well Wrought Urn.* New York, 1947.

Browning, Robert. *The Shorter Poems of Robert Browning.* Edited by William C. DeVane. New York, 1939.

Byron, Lord Gordon. *The Works of Lord Byron.* Edited by R. E. Prothero. London, 1922.

Cambridge Bibliography of English Literature, The. Edited by F. E. Bateson. London, 1941.

Campbell, Thomas. *The Poetical Works of Thomas Campbell.* Edited by W. A. Hill. Boston, 1854.

Churchill, Charles. *The Poems of Charles Churchill.* Edited by James Laver. London, 1933.

Cowper, William. *The Poetical Works of William Cowper.* Edited by H. S. Milford. London, 1934.

———. *William Cowper's Letters: A Selection.* Edited by E. V. Lucas. London, 1937.

Crabbe, George. *George Crabbe, Poems.* Edited by A. W. Ward. Cambridge, 1905-7.

――――. *The Poetical Works of the Rev. George Crabbe.* Edited by his son. London, 1834.

Denham, Sir John. *The Poetical Works of Sir John Denham.* Edited by T. H. Banks. New Haven, 1928.

Donne, John. *The Poems of John Donne.* Edited by H. J. C. Grierson. London, 1929.

Dryden, John. *The Works of John Dryden.* Edited by Scott and Saintsbury. Edinburgh, 1882.

Eliot, T. S. *Homage to John Dryden.* London, 1924.

――――. *The Sacred Wood.* London, 1928.

――――. *John Dryden, the Poet, the Dramatist, the Critic.* New York, 1932.

Elton, Oliver. *A Survey of English Literature, 1730-1780.* New York, 1928.

Forster, John. *Oliver Goldsmith.* London, 1871.

Gay, John. *The Poetical Works of John Gay.* Edited by G. C. Faber. London, 1926.

Gay, Phoebe. *John Gay: His Place in the Eighteenth Century.* London, 1938.

Goldsmith, Oliver. *The Poetical Works of Oliver Goldsmith.* Edited by Austin Dobson. London, 1927.

Huchon, René. *George Crabbe and his Times.* Translated by Frederick Clarke. London, 1907.

Hunt, Leigh. *The Poetical Works of Leigh Hunt.* Edited by H. S. Milford. London, 1923.

――――. *An Answer to the Question, 'What is Poetry?'* New York, 1926.

Irving, William. *John Gay, Favorite of the Wits.* Durham, N. C., 1940.

Johnson, Samuel. *The Poems of Samuel Johnson.* Edited by David Nichol Smith and Edward L. McAdam. Oxford, 1941.

Keats, John. *The Poems of John Keats.* Edited by E. DeSelincourt. London, 1926.

Krutch, Joseph W. *Samuel Johnson.* New York, 1944.

Leavis, F. R. *Revaluation.* London, 1936.

Melville, Lewis [pseud.]. *The Life and Letters of John Gay.* London, 1921.

Moore, Thomas. *The Poetical Works of Thomas Moore.* Collected by himself. London, 1840.

Pope, Alexander. *The Works of Alexander Pope.* Edited by Elwin and Courthope. London, 1871.

————. *The Rape of the Lock and Other Poems.* Edited by Geoffrey Tillotson. London, 1940.

Pound, Ezra. *Ezra Pound: Selected Poems.* Edited by T. S. Eliot. London, 1935.

Richards, I. A. *The Philosophy of Rhetoric.* New York, 1936.

Rogers, Samuel. *The Complete Poetical Works of Samuel Rogers.* Edited by Epes Sargent. Boston, 1854.

Root, Robert K. *The Poetical Career of Alexander Pope.* Princeton, 1938.

Sharp, Robert L. *From Donne to Dryden.* Chapel Hill, 1940.

Shelley, Percy B. *The Poems of Percy Bysshe Shelley.* Edited by C. D. Locock. London, 1911.

Sitwell, Edith. *Alexander Pope.* New York, 1930.

Smith, David Nichol. *Some Observations on Eighteenth Century Poetry.* London, 1937.

Tillotson, Geoffrey. *On the Poetry of Pope.* Oxford, 1938.

Tuve, Rosemond. *Elizabethan and Metaphysical Imagery.* Chicago, 1947.

Van Doren, Mark. *The Poetry of John Dryden.* New York, 1931.

Waller, Edmund. *The Poems of Edmund Waller.* Edited by G. T. Drury. London, 1893.

Warren, Austin. *Rage for Order.* Chicago, 1948.

Weber, Kurt. *Lucius Carey, Second Viscount Falkland.* New York, 1940.

Williamson, George. *The Donne Tradition.* New York, 1930.

Winters, Yvor. *In Defense of Reason.* New York, 1947.

Young, Edward. *The Poetical Works of Edward Young.* Edited by J. Mitford. Boston, 1854.

ARTICLES

Clark, Arthur M. "Thomas Heywood's *Art of Love* Lost and Found," *The Library*, 4th Series, III (Dec., 1922), 210-22.

Croker, John Wilson. "Endymion: A Poetic Romance," *The Quarterly Review*, XIX (April, 1818), 204-8.

Hill, Mary A. "Rhetorical Balance in Chaucer's Poetry," *Publications of the Modern Language Association*, XLII (Dec., 1927), 845-62.

Knapp, Mary E. Letter to *The Times Literary Supplement*, XLVI (Jan. 4, 1947), 9.

Knowlton, C. E. "The Origin of the Closed Couplet in English," *The Nation*, XCIII, N.S. (July 14, 1914), 134.

Lockhart, John G. "The Cockney School of Poetry," *Blackwood's Edinburgh Magazine*, III (Aug., 1818), 519-23

Schelling, Felix W. "Ben Jonson and the Classical School," *Publications of the Modern Language Association*, XIII (June, 1898), 221-50.

Shannon, George P. "Nicholas Grimald's Heroic Couplet and the Latin Elegiac Distich," *Publications of the Modern Language Association*, XLV (June, 1930), 532-42.

Tatlock, J. S. P. "The Origin of the Closed Couplet in English," *The Nation*, XCIII, N.S. (April 9, 1914), 390.

Wallerstein, Ruth. "The Development of the Rhetoric and Metre of the Heroic Couplet, Especially in 1625-1645," *Publications of the Modern Language Association*, L (March, 1935), 166-210.

Wasserman, Earl R. "The Return of the Enjambed Couplet," *Journal of English Literary History*, VII (1940), 239-52.

Weatherly, Edward H. "Churchill's Literary Indebtedness to Pope," *Studies in Philology*, XLIII (Jan., 1946), 59-70.

Williamson, George. "The Rhetorical Pattern of Neo-Classical Wit," *Modern Philology*, XXXII (August, 1935), 55-82.

Wimsatt, W. K., Jr. "One Relation of Rhyme to Reason," *Modern Language Quarterly*, V (Sept., 1944), 323-39.

Wood, Henry. "The Beginnings of the Classical Heroic Couplet," *American Journal of Philology*, XI (April, 1890), 55-79.

Index